Early Praise for

"*Abidance* should be required reading for anyone contemplating marriage. It is the most beautiful painting of love I have ever seen."
　　　　　– Carol Feller, author of *Dancing through Minefields*

"Whether you've been married for one year or seventy, this wonderful story will bring tears, laughter, and inspiration to your lives. A must for aging readers, which includes everyone."
　　　　　– Connie Shoemaker, author of *The Good Daughter: Secrets, Life Stories, and Healing*

"What a love story!"
　　　　　– Judith Macomber, Retired IT Analyst/Manager

"I truly adore this book. Lois has written a page-turner about two soul mates whose marriage has endured much struggle and yet have been blessed with boundless love and good times. In this day of social media and everything digital, this is a tale about something we often forget: The deep and abiding love two people can have for each other, and the life's journey they share."
　　　　　– Fred Silverman, New York Producer

"Lois has chosen her words in a wondrous fashion. I couldn't stop reading until I had turned the last page."
　　　　　– Arlo Sonnenberg, 100-year-old Renaissance Man

Other Books by Lois Tschetter Hjelmstad

Fine Black Lines: Reflections on Facing Cancer,
Fear and Loneliness

The Last Violet: Mourning My Mother,
Moving Beyond Regret

This Path We Share: Reflecting on 60 Years of Marriage

All four books are available online, from bookstores,
and at *www.loishjelmstad.com*

ABIDANCE

abide, v. – stand fast, sojourn, wait, accept

A Memoir of Love and Inevitability

Lois Tschetter Hjelmstad

Lois Tschetter Hjelmstad

*with much love
and best wishes!*

ABIDANCE

abide, v. – stand fast, sojourn, wait, accept

A Memoir of Love and Inevitability

Lois Tschetter Hjelmstad

Abidance
A Memoir of Love and Inevitability
by Lois Tschetter Hjelmstad

Copyright ©2019 by Lois Tschetter Hjelmstad

Published by
Mulberry Hill Press
2710 South Washington Street Suite B
Englewood, Colorado 80113-1679
www.mulberryhillpress.com

Editorial assistance: Barbara Munson
Cover and page design: Nick Zelinger
Cover photograph: Kara Hjelmstad

The following was originally published as indicated:
"No Lifeguard on Duty" in *Fine Black Lines: Reflections on Facing Cancer, Fear and Loneliness*, page 51

QuickBooks™ is a registered trademark of Intuit®
Name: Hjelmstad, Lois Tschetter, author.
Title: Abidance: a memoir of love and inevitability/
Lois Tschetter Hjelmstad.—1st Ed.
p.cm.

Identifiers: LCCN 2018944938 ISBN 978-0-9637139-0-2

Subjects: 1. Hjelmstad, Lois Tschetter. 2. Aging—Biography.
3. Marriage—Biography. 4. Family Relationships—Biography.
5. Caregivers—United States—Biographies. 6. Congestive Heart Failure—Biography. 7. Cancer—Patients—Biography 8. Loss (psychology)—Biography. 9. Anticipatory Grief—Biography. I. Title.

Printed in the United States of America

8 7 6 5 4 3 2 1

To Les
with whom I gratefully explore the
challenges and joys of
standing fast in the Age of Old-Old

It is the precise moment in which we concede our transience that life and love become most cherished.

– LTH

CONTENTS

FOREWORD

Love. We grow up dreaming about it. We spend our lives hoping to find it. Wars are fought over it. Countries are conquered for it. It's the warm sensation of a simple embrace and the unmatched feeling of utter exhilaration—the best part of life.

More than rainbows and butterflies, though, love can mean endurance through overwhelming hardship. Sometimes it's watching your life partner suffer terrible pain. It can be long nights in the hospital hoping your spouse wakes up. Days spent wondering if these are your last moments together on earth. Hours when you think the darkness will never end. Through it all, love endures.

I first met Les and Lois in the fall of 2015. I became their Primary Care Physician (PCP) when their former PCP transitioned to a new job. I remember our first appointment like it was yesterday. Les had a huge grin on his tan, friendly face. He greeted me with a hearty handshake. He was so genuinely optimistic. Lois had such an effortlessly caring way about her. She kept meticulous notes regarding his daily weights and vital signs. Her primary objective in life was clearly her husband's health, and her understanding of his medical conditions was far above average for a patient.

As a couple, Les and Lois are unmatched. They exude happiness, strength, perseverance, and persistence. They have the kind of love we all strive to get. This book shows us a piece of that love. Their love story will enhance our own.

Mark Andrew Nelson, MD

Denver, Colorado

Year 2008

The Winds of Time

*I feel the winds of time
brush by my face*

*The insistent breeze too rapidly
becomes
a relentless gale*

Sixty Years and Counting...

W e were as naïve as we were blissful.

We certainly knew about incredible love, but we were mere babes regarding inconceivable fear. We knew we were getting older, but we dismissed that knowledge as an inconvenient fact of life that hadn't touched our consciousness in any significant way.

And we were getting ready to celebrate our sixtieth wedding anniversary.

As the light began to fade from the Arizona sky on a beautiful September evening, my husband, Les, myself, and our four gray-haired children with their spouses—Karen, Bob and Vicki, Keith and Kara, Russ—gathered on Keith's patio.

Dozens of white candles floated on the pool; peals of laughter punctuated the chitchat; strains of *Mam'selle*, the 1947 hit that had become "our song," looped through the warm air. Dinner was over. Heartfelt toasts had been spoken. A bevy of desert quail perched on the back fence, waiting for darkness and rest.

It was time to renew our vows.

Les—still tall, still handsome, still vital—pulled a rumpled paper from his pocket and started to read:

My dear Lois Luene –
When I think of the words of our wedding vows, I recall love, cherish, and faithfulness. I feel I have lived

these words of commitment. There have been tough times. We have each needed—and granted—forgiveness. Our love for each other has been the one constant; it has invariably triumphed.

And now I promise you I will be at your side no matter what happens next. I will never abandon you or turn away from you. If I die before you, I will wait for you and I will love you forever.

I could hear the flutter of wings as the quail—one by one, two by two—glided from their roosts into the Texas ebony tree behind us. Soft coos began to calm the young ones for the night. Throaty murmurs mingled with the sniffles of the dear people who encircled us. I inhaled sharply and read:

My dearest sweetheart –

Sixty years ago, we chose to give our lives to one another. We forsook other possibilities and other opportunities. I feel incredibly blessed to have spent my life with you. I was crazy-in-love when we married and now after all these years I am still crazy-in-love with you.

So here on our sixtieth anniversary, I promise once again that I will remain by your side "until death do us part." I promise I will love you forever and, should I die before you, I will wait for you until the end of time.

Oh, yes, we said those fine words and we meant them from the bottoms of our hearts. They sound lovely to my ears to this very day. But, in retrospect, we could not yet fathom what our assurances meant.

Les and Lois on their wedding day,
September 12, 1948

Year 2012

Ninetieth Birthday

A glorious celebration
a fearsome thought
nine decades, each different
each flowing down the years
in a river of wonder, integrity, love

Let us not be afraid—

but immerse ourselves in gratitude
and grasp this moment
with joy

We're Almost Home

"He's dying. My husband is dying. Someone help us. Please. Someone. Anyone. Please."

My screams bounced off the windows of the train as we hurtled toward the Main Terminal at Denver International Airport the Sunday evening after Thanksgiving. My heart pounded, "How can I be losing my beloved husband? How can more than sixty-four years of marriage be ending on a damn train at DIA?"

———

We had deplaned at Gate B95—miles from where we needed to be to meet Bob's wife, Vicki. Les walked on the people mover and I trotted briskly beside him, getting my daily exercise. Les began walking slower and slower. Was his bad right knee bothering him that much?

"Honey, just ride," I suggested. I grabbed one of his bags, adding to the two I already carried.

He continued to struggle. When he stumbled off the people mover to join me, he gasped, "I can't go on. I *have* to sit down."

His face had turned from its normal ruddy tan to a pale bluish-gray. He looked so haggard that I checked for his pulse, "Where is it? I must have a bad spot. Why can't I get a pulse?"

A transport cart waited nearby, but the driver insisted that he was not authorized to leave the area to take us to the train.

"Maybe your husband can just sit on my cart and rest. Or there is a wheelchair station over there," he pointed off to the right.

"I don't think he can get there," I said. "Can you please give us a ride just that little way?"

We waited at the station four minutes before a young attendant came with a wheelchair. She took us down an elevator, then onto the train at Station B. As we sped toward Station A, I suddenly noticed that Les was staring into space.

Eyes wide open—nobody home.

I called to him, "Les. Sweetheart. Les, honey, wake up. *Please* wake up."

I shook him and shouted at him. No response. No heartbeat anywhere. One of his arms dropped to his side. Then the other fell.

My heart raced; bile rose in my throat; something in my chest contracted so I could hardly draw in air; the life force seemed to be seeping from my body and pooling on the dingy floor.

"My husband is dying. Please help me. Please help me." My voice fell to a whisper.

A man—another employee?—swooped in and whisked our wheelchair attendant and Les off the train. I jammed one of my suitcases into the door to keep it from closing with me inside. The train would have continued on, leaving Les on the other side.

I didn't know where we were. Our young attendant didn't know, either. She flailed her arms and whimpered, "Oh, God, I don't know what to do." The whisking man had disappeared.

Then I noticed wetness spreading in the crotch of Les' khakis. I had seen that happen once before when a friend had died. My fear, already beyond any I had ever experienced, soared higher than the spires of DIA.

I could see only one or two other people, but I continued to holler into the massive empty space. I clutched the arm of the lone passerby and begged him to help me lift Les to the floor so I could do CPR. We couldn't even budge his right leg.

Then Les moaned ever so slightly. My helper said, "See, he's okay. He doesn't need CPR, lady," and hurried off.

Someone had called the paramedics. When the seven strapping men arrived, the lead EMT put his stethoscope to Les' chest and said, "Your husband is very, very ill. An ambulance is coming." They carefully laid Les on the cold concrete floor. They started IVs and oxygen, working frantically. Les moaned once more.

The total despair that had washed over me began to ebb a little; a tiny ray of hope surged. Les was alive, but could he stay alive? Would he be the same person if he survived?

Somehow the ambulance driver and gurney men found us in the bowels of that huge airport. I called Vicki, who had been waiting in the forty-five-minute lot for over an hour and a half, apologized, outlined the situation, and told her where we were headed.

When we arrived at the ER of Porter Adventist Hospital, only four blocks from our house, Karen, Bob, and Vicki were already waiting in the dim lobby. Les slowly began to stabilize and become more lucid. I remained in his room overnight. Even tornado sirens could not have convinced me to leave; I had to stay with him, whatever happened.

As I tossed and turned on the hard, tapestry-covered pullout bench that served as a guest bed, I focused on how happy and secure we had been during the four years since our sixtieth anniversary.

Les had turned ninety in April, but we were living in our home of fifty-three years, cooking, gardening, entertaining family and friends as we had through the decades, loving our life together, and traveling.

It had been less than twelve hours since we said goodbye to Russ and his family after a wonderful holiday in Michigan. We had been excited to get home, to start Christmas preparations—putting up our three trees with the many tiny white bulbs, sending out cards, making caramel corn. So very happy....

Waiting for the Other Shoe

When we arrived home from the hospital the next afternoon, we missed our usual "Yay, we're home from our trip!" euphoria. I pulled our suitcases into the master bedroom and began to unpack. After five halfhearted minutes, I plopped down next to Les. We did not feel happy. Shell-shocked maybe. Yesterday morning seemed a long time ago. Christmas seemed a long way off.

The following day we saw our cardiologist, Dr. Hanson, for the first time. His reading glasses sat down on his nose and his crumpled white coat had seen better days, but he listened very carefully to us, then fitted Les with a heart rate monitor.

Les and I had convinced ourselves that Les had lost consciousness simply because he was dehydrated after a long day of travel.

I said, "We should have drunk water on the plane instead of that salty tomato juice. You may be ninety, but you can't possibly be ill."

"I'll wear this monitor just to humor the doctor. I'm going to be fine. You'll see," he said. I felt better.

As if to prove his normalcy, Les continued his usual activities—blowing leaves off the driveway, putting up the Christmas trees, helping me with a presentation at a homeless shelter, continuing our lifelong commitment to honor our marriage with physical intimacy—but he did not feel well. He was breathless; his heart raced too quickly at times, skipped beats and slowed almost to a halt at others.

A couple of days after the airport incident Les had his annual physical with our internist, Dr. Smith. Dr. Smith is a tall man with dark hair and a heavy beard, so obviously competent that no one could miss it. His empathy came through loud and clear, but I thought he seemed more concerned about Les than the situation warranted. I concentrated on enjoying the gorgeous Christmas decorations in the lobby.

A week later, I ran into the house to get the phone while Les carried in some groceries, one bag at a time. An agitated voice from the monitoring service said, "We've been trying and trying to reach you. You need to go straight to the ER. Mr. Hjelmstad is having extreme atrial fibrillation." We rushed over to Porter Hospital again.

Les' heart eventually resumed normal rhythm; we were home by suppertime. We both still considered the monitor a formality, an overabundance of caution, but a tiny barb of apprehension prickled the back of my neck.

Les went back to a-fibbing.

In the meantime, we zeroed in on following our Christmas traditions: the big family dinner on Eve-Eve; Christmas Eve with Karen's family; Christmas morning reserved for the two of us with seven gifts each plus a love letter.

In my note to Les, I questioned, "Is this the best? Is this the last? Or is this just another in a long string of Christmases? I do not know. But it is my clear chance to tell you once again how you keep me going, keep me safe, encircle me with love. I can only nestle in your arms, rest my cheek against yours, and treasure this moment."

On our fifth office visit since the airport, Dr. Hanson said, "This can't go on. Les needs a pacemaker and he needs it right away."

Over the years, my German heritage has left me with a strong predisposition to stoicism. But at that moment I was not a whit detached. Only gut-punched. My mouth dried. A wave of weakness flooded my core. I needed to focus and put on my advocacy hat.

During the thirteen words of Dr. Hanson's two devastating sentences, I switched places with the man who has always been my fortress.

Twenty-two years earlier, Les had cared for me after my breast cancer diagnosis: during my first mastectomy and radiation, then the second, then five other surgeries. And for twenty-three years he had been my solid backup as I coped with chronic fatigue syndrome (CFS).

Now one way or another I needed to muster my resources, dig deep for courage. Could I do it? Did I have a choice?

Les and I sat mutely in that office, overwhelmed. He reached for my hand and squeezed it. Almost before we could catch our breath or react, Dr. Hanson had dialed the electrocardiologist and scheduled surgery for January 4.

The Sunday after the airport incident our pastor had spoken of the Christian Advent Season as a time of waiting and grounding. He offered reassurances that, having coped with challenges in the past, we hold a resource for finding courage in the future.

Had the horror at the airport been some sort of preparation? A dress rehearsal, perhaps?

All I know is that I hope *never again* to feel as I had for those harrowing minutes.

But I also know that, in all probability, I will.

Year 2013

No Lifeguard on Duty

It is difficult
when one is drowning
to wave to the people
on shore

One wants to be
friendly, of course,

but perhaps it is
more important
to keep
swimming

Countdown

"It should be a routine procedure; however, he is ninety. It's a risk. But we have to do it." The doctor's parting words had not comforted us.

So five days before the surgery, in an attempt to quell my anxiety and calm myself, I reverted to my default position of writing my thoughts whenever my stress level gets too high. I'd been doing this for years.

I had written many poems and pieces during the early days of my breast cancer; they ultimately became a book, *Fine Black Lines: Reflections on Facing Cancer, Fear, and Loneliness.* As I wrote that book, I had struggled with the concept of taking care of myself even while I tried to keep those around me informed and comforted. One day, not making any headway in my writing, I asked Les to go for a walk with me so I could clear my mind.

All of a sudden, the words to "No Lifeguard on Duty" fell into my awareness, verbatim. We hurried home so I could write it down before I forgot. That poem has served as a mantra ever since. I felt as if I were drowning then. I was drowning again.

I sat down at my desk, and began to chart the days:

Five Days to Go

We got up earlier than usual and got to church later than usual, because we lingered over coffee too long. We had much to discuss, even after sixty-four years, three months, and nineteen days.

After church a friend asked about Les. I paused for a long moment and said, "He's getting a pacemaker on Friday. Simple, routine surgery. Until it's not."

Fourth Day

The nurse called to give prep instructions for the surgery. I dutifully wrote notes on a yellow pad. Then I said softly, "I know that to you he is a patient—an almost ninety-one-year-old patient—but to me he will always be twenty-six and I can't bear the idea of losing him."

That night, Les and I snuggled under our down comforter at nine-thirty, even though we usually stayed up for New Year's Eve. We held each other longer and more tightly than normal. He drew a pattern on my face with his finger and then kissed me, over and over.

Third Day

New Year's Day. We could have been making happy plans for the coming year, but we were stuck, not knowing if there would be a new year. How ironic to speculate whether our lives were over just as a new year began.

Even though it was a holiday, Les and I did our usual exercises before we got up. We routinely allow ourselves an extra thirty minutes in bed, if we spend that time stretching, exercising our legs, and lifting weights. A total con, but it works.

That day, our kitchen welcomed us with its beloved maple table that can be leafed to seat twelve people, the table that has hosted countless family celebrations.

Memories enfolded us as we sat down for breakfast: four young children, two of them sitting on phone books so they could reach their plates; later the four teens huddled over homework; the "last breakfast" as each of them left for college.

The remainder of the day I worked on my long-scheduled talk for the next morning. My book, *Fine Black Lines*, had opened doors for me to speak to support groups, medical personnel, students, and large conferences in all fifty states, Canada, and England. Over 600 talks and counting.

And the mastectomy picture I had included in that book led to my appearing, naked from the waist up, showing my scars, on the cover of *Colorado Woman News* back in the time when no one was so bold. Many survivors and caregivers thanked me for displaying the hidden.

In my speaking, Les and I had found a way to be useful in the breast cancer community. One doctor told us that we needed to keep on keeping on.

As I worked, I wondered how this new wrinkle in our lives would impact that long, accidental career as we tried to go forward.

Second Day

We got up early to get ready for my speech. Les felt weak, shaky, and nauseated.

"Are you *sure* we can do this today?" I asked.

"Oh, yeah, I think so. I feel fine when I'm driving," he said, "and I love sitting there listening to you. You always sparkle."

During that talk, I sent Les a special smile as I read one of the passages that had been written specifically for him. He smiled back with that same beautiful smile that had captured my heart. He looked a bit wan and his eyes looked tired, but his face glowed with purpose and pride.

We were doing our work, together, and to both of us it felt good. Normal. It was not a time to think about surgery.

Last Day

"Shall we do something special? A movie, perhaps?" I asked quietly.

"No, let's just live. I love our life," he sighed.

Day of Surgery

Bob, Vicki, and Karen plus her grown children, Doug and Emily, joined me to huddle together at St. Joseph Hospital.

When Dr. Porter, the electrocardiologist, came in, we all gasped. With his slight build, curly hair, and quick step, he looked way too young. He assured us that he had done this many, many times, but when an orderly wheeled Les away, I cried.

A nurse directed us to the stark surgical waiting room where the smudged gray walls, worn carpet, listless volunteer, and stale coffee did not inspire confidence or comfort us. The smell of fear mingled with the sting of powerful antiseptic.

But, quite a bit later, when Dr. Porter returned from the OR to tell us that Les had come through as well as could be expected, the dreary room seemed less dismal.

As I breathed easier and looked around, I noticed the painting of a beautiful landscape that I had missed before.

A Night to Remember

That night as I tried to sleep on a hard faux leather recliner next to Les' bed, a flimsy pea green blanket barely covering my toes, my mind churned with recollections of our long life together:

How amazing that we had been married over sixty-four years. How improbable that a willful seventeen-year-old and a WWII vet could hammer out a true marriage. And how unlikely that we had even met. It was one of those weird butterfly effects.

What if my great-grandfather had not left Crimea to find religious freedom in South Dakota, where I was born in the same year that Les turned eight?

What if his grandparents had not migrated from Norway? What if his oldest brother, Magnar, had not left the homestead in North Dakota, run out of money 893 miles later, met and married a nice Colorado girl? What if, seven years later, his next brother, Harold, had not visited Magnar, met Doris, another nice Colorado girl, and married her? What if, seven years after that, Les, just discharged from the Navy, had not visited Harold? And what if my family had not moved to Denver? Not joined Harold's church? What if Doris had not invited our family for Thanksgiving dinner in 1946?

Would Les have found me anyway?

I didn't know then, of course, that Les had been BMOC (Big-Man-on-Campus) in his small Ryder High School— lettering four years in football, captain of the team; lettering in basketball for three years; going out for track; and presiding over his senior class.

And he didn't know that I was Denver South High School's IGOCWOAT (Invisible-Girl-on-Campus-Wallflower-of-All-Time). Or that I would graduate valedictorian of my class of 721, but no one would notice.

We didn't date until the following June, right after I finished my junior year. We got engaged in October. We married eleven months after that; I was almost eighteen.

The first two years we lived and worked for $150 a month on a chicken ranch. We cherished being married and loved the farm, but we couldn't afford to stay there, even though I returned almost immediately to the insurance underwriting job I had left to get married. Forget the post-WWII mores of married women staying at home; we needed money.

We moved back into Denver. Les took a job at Gates Rubber Company, where he worked for thirty-seven years, twenty-six of them on night shift, most of them as a supervisor.

Karen was born the day before I turned twenty-one. Bob, Keith, and Russ followed. What a smart move it was to have four children and how clever to have had them two years apart. They fit nicely around a card table when they played Monopoly. And although I've heard that children are never an unmixed blessing, we are extraordinarily grateful for each of ours.

Meanwhile, Les' next younger brother, Ralph, married Mary Jo. The four of us became best friends. They were our go-to couple for diversion, counsel, and consolation. Our four children and their three girls grew up together.

I began teaching Bobby piano when he was seven; Karen and I were already taking lessons; we couldn't pay for additional ones. Neighborhood kids and others joined in. I took a number of college pedagogy courses to become a better teacher. That inadvertent career encompassed hundreds of students and lasted almost forty years.

I planned to teach until I was ninety-six even though Les retired at sixty-five, returned to college, and earned a degree. But then there was that breast cancer thing, my first book, and the whole unplanned speaking career.

Since I had written one book, why not another? Or two? Or three?

As I fidgeted in that miserable hospital recliner that night, trying to get comfortable, pretty much reviewing our entire life together, one of the things that stood out was how hard the two of us had worked. We didn't know much about "Me Time."

But the other thing that became obvious was that we hadn't minded. We adored one another. We wanted to be together. We planned a family of four children. Then we had proceeded to do what it took to make it work.

Now, somehow, we needed to figure out how to make this work.

I fell asleep just as the day nurses came in to debrief. We were home by noon.

Now, *now*, we would go back to normal.

Everything would be fine.

Not Quite So Fast!

Everything would be fine?

Two weeks later Les and I braved the icy roads and returned to Dr. Porter's office for the post-surgical and device check-up.

"Oh, no," Dr. Porter said, as he checked the readout of the new pacemaker, "you've continued to a-fib. Clearly your post-surgery medication is not working well."

We sat dumbfounded. Les had been gallantly running little errands and helping me clean the house. He had agreed to the surgery. Surely it had made him better.

The doctor gave us a new prescription.

The next day, as I made our bed, I watched my love from across the room, sitting in his recliner, eyes closed, arms limp. A sense of helplessness engulfed me. What could I do to help him? How could I keep myself strong enough to cope? I tried to be philosophical, tried to find some optimism, tried to raise the level of cheer in our household, but the facts kept barging in.

Les continued to a-fib every day; he felt terrible—sick to his stomach, weak, woozy, winded. He endured the side effects of his new medication for six weeks. He tried another. And another.

The first week in May, as we undressed for bed, Les showed me his right leg, purple, badly swollen from his toes to his knee. We threw on our clothes and went to the Porter

ER. His blood was way too thin; the doctors insisted that he stay the night. I stayed with him, of course.

The medication trials and the negative side effects continued until around the first of June when Les said, "No more. No more. I'd rather die than take medicine that makes me feel this sick. I want to live my life."

The doctor decided to try a "pill-in-the-pocket" approach. Les was to take it only when his heart rate went sky high.

Father's Day

*D*earest sweetheart –

Now, after all these years, I have to admit that I was not thinking of you as a father when I agreed to spend my life with you. It was sheer love and longing that drove me into your arms. What a pleasant surprise it has been to discover that you are a superb husband and father.

Although it was quite a bit more fun making babies than delivering them, I hold dear the memories of your sitting by me during four labors, stroking my damp hair, holding my hand, breathing with me, telling me I was magnificent. After our first two premature babies, it meant everything to me that you were as eager to use natural childbirth for our last two children as I was. It went well.

When Karen was two, you frequently washed her silky golden hair. I can picture your sturdy square hands tipping her back over the sink.

"I'll be gentle," you said.

She replied, "What does 'gentle' mean?"

Years later, you took Karen and her friends to football games, good-naturedly tolerating the shrieks and giggles of a car full of teenage girls.

It pleased me to watch you bathe the scrawny little boy bodies, wrap them in towels, and hold them in your strong arms. *You frequently played catch with them and let them help you with things around the yard, rarely allowing your patience to grow thin. Once you stayed up until three a.m. to talk our youngest out of buying a motorcycle.*

You were the steady one in parenting, calming my freak-out when our three thought-to-be-reliable boys had a raucous party, spilled beer all over the carpet, shampooed it, then set furniture on it while it was wet—all just before you and I returned home from a trip to Canada. You'll remember that we didn't leave home again until those three were out of the house permanently.

You worked hours and hours of overtime to keep our family afloat during tough times. When you finished your night shift, you walked, tall and straight, through the back door into the kitchen at seven-thirty. Your eyes were sunken and tired, but your mouth spread into a radiant "I'm-so-glad-to-see-you-all" smile.

When I was in the hospital for twenty-three days after a surgery gone wrong, you visited me every day while you took care of our children and worked.

And you are the man who provides clear counsel to those four grown children, even today.

What I'm trying to say is that we all lucked out. Thank you, father of my children, thank you, thank you, thank you.

Love, Mam'selle

Unsteady

Toward the end of June, Les came into the kitchen from the patio where he had set the fire for our evening cookout. A trickle of blood ran down his right cheek and dripped onto the hardwood floor.

"I'm so darn awkward! I tried to step onto the deck and fell against the brick wall," he said.

I grabbed a tube of ointment and three adhesive strips, cleaned his face, and repaired the ragged triangular tear on his forehead.

Several weeks later, in the dark of the night, Les went to the bathroom. As he fumbled his way back to bed, he fell against the cedar chest and broke his sternum. The break caused him pain for eight weeks or so, adding to his misery.

These accidents reminded me of injuries he had sustained in a car accident long ago—concussion, broken neck, fractured pelvis, one ear barely hanging. He was in the hospital two weeks, then in my care for many more. His young doctor told me not to be upset: Les had had a good life.

Les was *fifty-nine*.

Although he hadn't ever been laid up as long as that, he had come even closer to death in a freak factory accident when Russ was a baby.

Les had indeed recovered well in the past, but he was ninety-one now. The frequency of his current mishaps frightened me. He continued to say that it was okay, he would be okay, but I saw his unsteadiness as a problem.

Each hot summer day, as July wandered into August, I clung to my stoicism, my pragmatism, doing whatever needed doing, falling into bed in sheer exhaustion every night.

It was as if Les were climbing a tall ladder and I held it, hoping to keep it stable.

The New Car

"Careful on those steps, Dad." Karen took Les' arm as we walked into the house. "Don't try to carry the groceries. I'll bring them in." She always watched her dad warily, ready to take hold of him, ready to admonish, if necessary.

It was obvious that our devoted, intelligent children worried about Les—and me. They helped whenever they could; they were protective; they wondered whether perhaps it might be time to help us manage our affairs. I understood.

When my parents were only in their seventies, I was convinced I needed to watch over them; to me they were old. I devoured articles in *AARP* magazines: *What to Do about Elderly Parents, How to Have the Driving Conversation, Only You Can Keep Your Parents Safe.* I even used some of the advice.

On the other hand, Les, our doctor, and I agreed that we were capable of assessing our situation and searching for solutions. In fact, the doctor encouraged us, insisting that it was important that we stay as active and engaged as possible. Les and I wanted to be as independent as we could. The fact that we sometimes needed help frustrated us.

Meanwhile, our kids tried to fulfill what they perceived to be their obligations. They were especially concerned about Les driving in his weakened condition.

Tensions arose.

So I was surprised early in August when Les announced, "Let's go look at new cars. Ours is already four years old." He touched my arm gently. "And when I die you need to have a reliable new one so you don't have to even think about cars."

I didn't want to think about cars *or* dying, but I went with him to three dealerships. At the first place, Les looked at one car, leaned against it, and soon went back to our car to sit down. What? He had always loved looking at cars. I walked around the other lots and reported back to him. When we got home, I searched online. There simply weren't any Honda Accords with the equipment and color we wanted available in Colorado.

Maybe we should forget it. Not cause angst.

Les was not to be deterred. Three days later he drove us over to AAA. The car salesman doubted that he could locate what we wanted. Inventory was low. But when he checked, the exact one we sought had just unloaded at a dealership in Boulder. We thought it over—for about seven seconds. That model had a backup camera, a right-lane camera, and GPS plus collision and line-crossing warnings.

"Wonderful. Wonderful! Now you'll always have a reliable car," Les said. "You'll be safe."

Find Joy

A week after that Les gave in to his physical therapist's pleas and began using a cane to alleviate the arthritis pain, deformation, and bone-against-bone in his right knee. He was too old and too sick to have a replacement. However, the cane seemed to further undermine his confidence and distort his sense of personhood, reminding him daily of his aging, illness, and disability.

In our denial and desperation to "get back to normal," we made a plan to drive our new car to Arizona at the end of August.

We had first traveled to the Valley of the Sun during my piano studio's spring break in 1973. It rained the entire week, but the unique vegetation and landscape fascinated us.

Ralph and Mary Jo moved to Phoenix the next year. Then Les and I visited them every March for more than forty years.

When Keith, Kara, and their three kids located to Mesa in 2008, we began going down each and every time we could.

We love Arizona.

But it turned out that Les was too sick to go at the end of this August. He was so disappointed that I felt obligated, nay burdened, to make some sort of alternate plan.

"Well," I reasoned, "he hasn't quite recovered, but surely we can make our annual November trip. I'll go ahead and buy the tickets; everything will work out."

I went online; we would fly on November 4.

That happy plan made, we looked forward to our sixty-fifth anniversary coming up mid-September.

Our children treated us to an extravagant weekend at the Grand Hyatt Hotel in downtown Denver. Les couldn't walk any distance, so they hired Pedicabs to carry us.

Les and I had compiled a quiz of sixty-five questions about our marriage, the years when the kids were home, and old family stories. Riveted, our children wrote fast and furiously, compared notes, and laughed uproariously at every time-worn joke.

The only glitch occurred the second evening. As we were taking pictures in front of the restaurant, Les almost fainted. The boys managed to half drag him across the gaudy flowered carpet to a private dining cove, where I stretched him out on the floor until he had recovered enough to sit up and eat his dinner. He laughed later, "It wasn't all bad. Our waitress wore a very short skirt."

Our Big Bash anniversary weekend exceeded all expectations. We put aside what lay behind and refused to ponder what might lie before us.

And we remembered once again that joy and sorrow often occupy the same space.

Our Walk

We have always walked together
side by side
hand in hand
step matching step

Now I walk alone—
your knee, you know,
too stiff to function, too old to replace—

I borrow your cane
it's not the same

Oktoberfest

Two weeks after our anniversary, Les and I figured we would risk an outing over Squaw Pass to Echo Lake Lodge in celebration of my eighty-third birthday. We had visited the Lodge so often that we were dear friends with the owner, Barb Day. She greeted us heartily, reached out for big hugs, and insisted I take a birthday present from the gift shop. I deliberated between earrings and Echo Lake Lodge mugs. I chose two of the latter.

The little excursion enchanted us. At the very peak of their color, the aspen trees shimmered in the soft breeze. Smoke curled from wood-burning stoves and evoked memories of special mountain holidays. Les loved taking his new car onto the highway and revving it up. It purred.

On the way back we stopped at an overlook we had long considered to be ours.

⁓

In the spring and summer before our thirty-third anniversary, Les and I fell into a four-month funk about our marriage. Even though we made love at the promised regular intervals, we could not communicate in actual conversation. We were miserable. One day the ugly word divorce was tossed out into the coldness.

Finally, late in July 1981, the day Prince Charles married Diana, we drove up toward Echo Lake Lodge, pulled off at a spot we had frequently visited and found our favorite log. We weren't talking, but we took a seat together and inhaled the clear mountain air. All of a sudden Les reached over and pulled me close. And we talked.

We relived some of the high and low points of our marriage; we made plans.

We understood that throwing away our rich history together would be beyond absurd.

We reactivated the love that lay just beneath the icy surface of no communication, waiting for us to remember.

From that day on we seldom argued or yelled or slept on the couch. We understood our marriage as a gift to be appreciated and cared for gently. In our perseverance, the love we shared from the beginning had prevailed. What if we had missed all these additional years?

~

And there we were, once again sitting on our log, savoring the view. After the ten tough months of illness and doctoring we had just weathered, we felt alive and real. We presumed that the worst was over; Les was only ninety-one, he could live to be one hundred and three. We decided to relax and enjoy life. It had been hard, but it was better.

And we had that November trip to anticipate.

Five Percent or So

Six days later, Les woke me in the night, "I can't breathe; I can't breathe. Help me. Please." I jumped out of bed. There he sat in his recliner, pale, ashy, and freaked. His terror seized me.

I told myself, "Calm down. Calm down. You can take care of this."

I helped him pull on his sweatpants and drove to our same old Porter Hospital ER.

After many blood draws, much consternation, and IV medication to draw off the fluid that had built up, the young hospitalist reported that the tests indicated congestive heart failure (CHF). I shuddered, but I was quite sure that someone had made a mistake.

Right after I had thus comforted myself, she asked what they should do in case Les coded. Coded? CPR? Ventilator?

Somehow I had the presence of mind to ask what the chances were, once heroic measures had been employed, of getting back my same husband.

She quietly said, "Only five percent or so."

I scrounged around for a piece of paper. Even though I had his Medical Power of Attorney in my purse, Les insisted on writing "no resuscitation or ventilator." He shakily signed the tiny scrap. I sat there with my head in my hands.

The doctor admitted Les for observation; I slept in his room on a pullout bench and covered myself with my down comfort coat. We went home the next evening without a prescription; he had already tried all of the possible medications.

Three weeks later our internist confirmed that Les indeed had congestive heart failure. My whole body tightened. It wasn't that I was unaware: the airport episode, the pacemaker, the continuing physical decline. How could I not be aware?

But that day it hit me hard. Maybe it was because I had been editing the Kindle edition of the book about my mother's dying. Perhaps it was because I had finally had the courage to go to Google, where I learned that heart failure is terminal, that the final path can be horrendous.

Les continued to get sicker. The last day of October, after a month of continuous heart rates near 150, Dr. Hanson decided that we had no choice other than to do the AV (atrioventricular) node ablation that he had been trying hard to avoid. He called Dr. Porter again, who scheduled the surgery for November 4, the day we were to have flown to Phoenix.

Neither Les nor I could believe that he was facing another worrisome anesthetic, another messing around with his heart, another road of recovery. We sat there in the office, avoiding one another's eyes, trying to keep our composure.

I cancelled our plane tickets.

On the day of surgery, the family and I once again sat in the waiting room at St. Joe's. When Les was finally back in his room and everyone had had a chance to say "hi" and hug him, I sent them home. I didn't feel like visiting; Les needed to rest. A great deal of relief and gratitude flooded over me that he had made it through another surgery. But would that help his heart? What would be next? After an emotionally and physically exhausting day, Les and I had a quiet evening.

By the next night Les and I were home again, sitting near the gas fireplace in our bedroom, discussing when to put up our Christmas trees, reviewing the events of the year almost past, and wondering...

Why aren't the lifeguards on duty? How do we keep swimming now?

And how do we move forward and live the last years of such a long marriage, such a deliberate marriage, such an entwinement of lives?

Christmas 2013

*D*earest sweetheart –

While this Christmas probably has been one of our best, it also has been one of our saddest. It is hard to see how we can be given another.

When I think back, I can't quite remember where this nightfall of our lives began.

I do remember that when you and I were married over sixty-five years ago, just three years after the United States dropped A-bombs on Hiroshima and Nagasaki, we clung to the hope that we would have five years together before the world blew up.

And I remember awaking early one Sunday some sixteen years later, watching you sleep quietly beside me during your only night off that week. I suddenly sat up, struck by an unwelcome concept: He is forty-two. If he lives to be eighty-four (an unimaginable number), today his life is half over. I reached out to touch your cheek.

Then there was the day you turned fifty-six and my mind searched for all those years since I first saw you and forever lost my heart. My image of you suddenly flipped to reality. Light-headedness engulfed me.

But when did this begin? This fright, this darkness, this unthinkable awareness that drifts over and around me like layered black smoke from a too-hot fire? When did this time of waiting, standing fast, abiding start?

When did I first notice the long shadow of goodbye creeping up behind us?

Was it your ninetieth birthday almost two years ago?

Was it last fall when Bob offered, "I'll do your yard next season, Dad. In fact, I'll do it the rest of your life."

You had leaned against the gate then and, much to my disbelief, agreed.

Was it that horrifying November evening at the Denver International Airport? Was it the emergency room visits, the medication trials, the months of worsening illness?

I don't really know when it began.

I don't remember when my original wedding prayer of "Please let us have just five years" morphed into notions that "Maybe this love is forever."

I'm not sure when my perception moved on to "Better brace yourself. This is not going to last a whole lot longer."

How did we get here? Surprised and dismayed?

I can't wrap my mind around any of this. Even though you are almost ninety-two, it feels unreal. Most of the time I try to stay in denial because otherwise my lungs freeze and I can't breathe.

Time has flown swiftly. In my mind and heart you are my twenty-six-year-old newly-minted husband. That is, until I look closely and see your emaciated arms and legs, your ankles and calves so swollen that I had to order super stretchy sox; until I listen carefully and hear your labored breathing and wistful sighs; until I lie in your arms and feel my heart shatter into a thousand fragments as it listens to yours trying to keep up.

   I love you.

      Mam'selle

Year 2014

Going, Going...

Day by day he disappears
skin and muscle shriveling
I always thought he was big-boned

but now I see
he isn't

Another Chink in the Armor

Les shambled into the kitchen while I was making breakfast on a Tuesday mid-January. It had been two months since his AV surgery.

"I'm really sick," he panted as he held on to the back of a chair, needing support even though he had already rested in the living room, halfway between the bedroom and kitchen.

"More than usual?" I asked.

"Really ill."

"What's different?"

"I can barely catch my breath. I'm nauseated and almost unbearably weak."

I helped him sit down. He took two small bites, then laid his toast back on the plate.

I watched him carefully through that day and the next, hoping to wait until his scheduled post-op appointment in two days. He continued to be breathless at the slightest exertion, but not more so.

Karen met us at Dr. Porter's office on Thursday. The doctor welcomed us with a big smile.

"Everything's going well?" he asked as he placed his cold stethoscope on Les' bare chest.

Les preferred to encourage his nice doctor, but I had urged him to forget the brave face this time.

"Not so great."

"Hmm. Hmm. Did you have this loud heart murmur before? I don't recall hearing it," the doctor said with a frown. "We'd better do an echocardiogram." He listened again, more intently. "Hmm. If this is what I think it is, and if the ECHO confirms it, I think we can fix it, but I'm very, very hesitant to do additional surgery."

Something in my stomach dropped to the bottom of my toes. If we were lucky, maybe another surgery. And if another surgery, there would be another period of recovery. And if this wasn't what he thought....

Be My Valentine

Three weeks later, February 10, Les and I got up at four-fifteen, at least four hours earlier than usual, and Vicki drove us down to St. Joseph Hospital.

The registration and prep time seemed much like the same old, same old of prior excursions. The surgical waiting room looked same old, same old, too. I worked two Jumbles, six Sudoku, and nine crossword puzzles. I was too distraught to chat with Karen, Bob, and Vicki. I knew that, in his condition, Les should not be having even the tiniest bit of anesthesia. It was too dangerous.

After two and a half hours, the puzzles no longer distracted me. Suddenly nothing was same old. Time continued to pass. I paced the waiting room. I thought, "This is taking longer than the doctor said." The sick, familiar fear that perhaps Les would not come out of this surgery wedged itself into my consciousness. I bent over gagging.

Finally, Dr. Porter came out and said that the procedure had been successfully completed—although it had been more challenging than he had expected. There had been very worrisome moments.

I exhaled.

I slept on the same hard faux leather recliner that night, watched the heart monitor, and listened to the music of the new steady thump. The next afternoon Karen brought us home—Les with a sore chest and me with a very bruised, but relieved, heart.

Only time would tell if this new biventricular pacemaker would disrupt his heart failure sufficiently. We were trying to be cautiously hopeful.

But I grew ever more aware of our mortality—especially his—and in three days, it would be Valentine's Day.

On Valentine's Les set a beautiful card, lacy with pink glitter, by my place at breakfast. He had had it all planned before he went to surgery. In my anxious state, I had done nothing for him. But that evening I dashed off a quick poem:

You've said so much in your beautiful card
and I've also said it before
but I can't let this day just fade into night
and not let you know this once more—
You're my pillar of strength, my wings of support,
my old ship of life's only shore
your most loving smile and arms ever strong
are things I completely adore

So be happy, my darling, in unending love
and if you should travel before
be waiting, my sweet, your arms still outstretched
right by that welcoming door

It won't be heaven without you

Mam'selle

To Drive or Not to Drive

A week or so later, driving home from another doctor visit, I rounded the northwest corner of Downing and Yale without hitting the curb.

Les said, "Nice one. You are such a good driver."

He frequently said that to encourage me. Even though he taught me to drive the summer before we were married, when I was seventeen, he had been the chief driver in our household. Of course, I had ferried kids as often as anyone, but I never drove if I could help it.

"It's dear of you to notice," I laughed.

Les had voluntarily agreed not to drive while he was so ill, starting the day after our trip to Echo Lake Lodge, even though he had been a skillful, intrepid driver for most of his life. I had always felt completely safe with him at the wheel.

Having driven so rarely in the more than twenty years since Les retired, it took me a while to become comfortable with it again. I often glanced at my hands on the steering wheel and exclaimed, "I can't *believe* I'm driving."

By the time Les' health had stabilized to the point that he could reconsider driving, our children definitely did not want him to resume. Sometimes they hinted; sometimes they yelled.

The circumstances jammed me into a dreadful quandary because I could feel how desperately Les longed to drive; I could see how many ways in which it would make him feel whole again; he lamented not driving each time we got in the car. But I knew that neither of us could endure reading an item in *The Denver Post* that said something about a ninety-plus-year-old man with heart issues losing control of his car and....

I kept driving. I did not mind traffic or going into downtown Denver, but I avoided the Interstate, which ruled out the two of us going on any sort of road trip. Even if Les could have traveled. Or the kids would have agreed.

Basically, we were...

Grounded

One midafternoon in late February, Les and I sat by the kitchen table, drinking peach tea, eating dark chocolates, hoping to engage in some teasing and light-hearted banter.

We tried.

But that day we couldn't quite manage chitchat. Les did not feel well. He had hoped his surgery earlier in February would have helped more, sooner.

He told me once again that he was not afraid to die, that he was content that he had lived according to his values, that he had loved his life. He quoted the Bible verse that was his lifelong watchword:

> *What doth the Lord require of thee, but to*
> *do justly, and to love mercy, and to walk*
> *humbly with thy God?* – Micah 6:8

We shared our sadness in knowing that the days ahead were many fewer than the sixty-five years behind. Even if Les rallied for another four or five years, our long marriage would not last indefinitely. As we contemplated the unimaginable, a wrenching pain moved into my heart. Les sighed.

In an effort to divert myself, I set down my cup and glanced at the mail I had brought in earlier. Three travel brochures—*Brekke, Globus Tours,* and *Viking River Cruises*—popped up in the stack of ads, catalogues, and bills.

I used to love looking at the various tours. A year or so ago I would have spent the rest of the afternoon dreaming up possible trips.

But now...

Since the night in the airport, fifteen months ago, we had been essentially homebound. We, whose lives had revolved around the next trip, had gone only to the grocery store and appointments. We, who had not missed a Sunday in years, had been to church three times in eight months. We, who had visited our family and friends frequently, now had occasional dinners brought in.

Who could have dreamed that we would spend two quiet winters in our little red brick house?

Abruptly getting grounded on the day Les passed out in the airport—on the way home from a classic trip to visit our youngest son—was not exactly how we had planned to structure the remainder of our lives.

Even before I had breast cancer and had written *Fine Black Lines*, even before we covered 400,000 miles on speaking tours, travel had been the way we lived. We visited our far-flung children and grandchildren frequently, making it a point to attend every graduation—high school, GED, BAs, MAs, PhDs, DMAs, and MDs.

And for years, we had hoped to stretch our lives far enough to see our two youngest granddaughters, Kirsten and Annika, graduate from high school. Could Les live until ninety-two and ninety-three? We had never even *known* anyone that old.

I set our empty teacups in the sink, then briefly leafed through the travel brochures. Tears stung my eyes, trickled through my mascara, and dripped off my chin.

Snatching those happy, colorful pamphlets, I stepped into the garage and pitched them into the large gray recycle bin.

I could not be sure that we would ever travel again or that we would even continue to be "we."

Shopping Trip

"I love this brushed steel watch with its black face. And it has large numerals. It will be perfect for my husband." I set down my packages and wiped a small tear. "His birthday is in six weeks, but I'm going to give it to him now. I'm not sure he will live until then."

The clerk looked up at me. "Oh, my goodness," she said.

"Will you trust me to take the watch out to the car for him to try on, so we can size the band? I can't get him in here. He's too ill to walk that far."

I went to the car where Les sat with Keith and his son, David, who were visiting over spring break. Since Keith could drive and wait with Les, I had taken the opportunity to go to a distant mall to pick up some foundation and lipstick in Dillard's.

"For me? Really? This is so *exciting!*" Les said as he fumbled with the clasp.

His watch had broken months earlier; things had been too chaotic to take time to get it repaired. Besides, Les had told me that I shouldn't worry about it—he probably wouldn't need it for long, anyway. That remark reminded me of the decision he had made in regard to his teeth. His practical side would not allow him to put the monetary equivalent of a fancy new car into a ninety-one-year-old mouth when a $1000 denture would serve the purpose just fine, thank you.

But as I darted past the jewelry section on my way to cosmetics, I suddenly realized how ridiculous it was that I had listened to him. Maybe an expensive mouth didn't make sense, but why shouldn't Les have a beautiful new watch, even if he only used it days or weeks?

Keith and David estimated how many links needed to be removed to fit his skinny arm.

When I ran back into the store, the clerk, looking sad, shortened the band.

Waterfall

In mid-April, as we sipped coffee and watched a late spring snow blanket our tulips, we mused how March had been as bleak as February. Les' recovery seemed slow or nonexistent. The weather had been unpleasant all spring. We had rarely left the house. Every day when I awoke, I touched Les to see if he was warm and looked closely to see if his chest rose and fell.

Recently he had said three or four times that he felt as if he were dying. I always shushed him and told him not to say things like that, but I could easily see how discouraged he was.

Just as I was hoping our conversation would turn a tad brighter, a waterfall of questions cascaded onto the table:

"How will it be in the last days?

"Will I suffocate?

"Will it be sudden or excruciatingly slow?

"How will you manage the yard when I'm gone?"

As a laid-back Norwegian and stoic German, neither of us has been noted for crying, but I burst into tears. Les slid his chair around the table and drew me into his arms. He pressed his wet cheeks against mine.

How can we hold incredible love and inconceivable fear in our hearts at the same time?

Bucket List Revisited

A week after that torrent of tears, we sat in the comfort of our warm bedroom—Les in his red plaid pajamas, I with my teal fleece robe wrapped tightly.

"Anything special you'd like to do for your ninety-second birthday?" I asked. "It's only two weeks away."

"Well, I'd prefer to go on an African safari, but I doubt that's in the cards," Les chuckled as he continued, "and I certainly can't jump out of a plane like George H. W. I guess the only thing left on our actual Bucket List is to get to Mesa next month for Kirsti's graduation."

It had been eighteen months since we last visited Mesa, just prior to the horror at the airport we'd had and the ensuing medical issues. While our travel days appeared over, in reality we weren't quite finished.

Right there at the top of our list was that long-standing tradition of attending graduations. Kirsten would graduate high school in May. Her sister, Annika, would graduate the following spring. If we could somehow get there this year, maybe we could combine the commemorations. We certainly didn't feel we could count on next year.

In January Keith and Kara had invited us to spend the winter months with them and stay for the graduation, but Les couldn't get well enough to travel out of Denver.

Every time we asked the doctor, he'd say, "Not yet. Not yet. We have to get Les better."

Our children contended that, if we went, someone needed to accompany us. They are busy people; that would be logistically difficult. No one, not even I, the inveterate traveler, could visualize the two of us out on the road alone.

I had wondered if perhaps Les could recover a bit of energy and breathe better at the lower altitude. I fervently wished to test that theory.

We were also anxious to see Ralph, Les' brother, who had suffered a stroke. He had not done well since Mary Jo died six years earlier.

Our beloved Dr. Smith knew about the offer, the gravitational pull of the graduation, and our need to see Ralph. He and we had discussed possible scenarios at every two-week follow-up visit all winter. Les and I knew he would okay a trip if he could.

The last week of April he finally said, "Yes. Yes. Yes, but only if you go by car and if someone takes you. We all know it's a risk, but I believe it is one worth taking."

By the Time We Get to Phoenix

The second Thursday in May dawned cold and rainy with a stiff wind. After a quick breakfast, Les and I sat on the sofa waiting for our transportation.

I said, "Isn't it ironic that we need a ride? Wouldn't it be great to just hop in our own car and shoot down the highway like we have hundreds of times before?"

Bob and Vicki arrived at 9:50, stowed our suitcases, the down comforter, and the nineteen-pound transport chair in their SUV, and we were off at 9:59, one minute early. "That's what we're looking for," our CPA son said, "precision."

We passed Colorado Springs, then Pueblo. The weather got nastier, the wind colder. Every time we made a bathroom stop, Bob almost had to carry Les.

I had to wonder, "How did we ever think this was a good idea? What are we doing? We are miles and miles from a hospital. We barely got the okay from Dr. Smith in time to make this trip. Sure, we're on the way to Phoenix, but at what cost?"

I was so worried that my tummy hurt.

In my view from the left rear seat, I observed Les riding shotgun. He watched the road every second as if sixty-year-old Bob had never driven before. I noticed how thin his neck was, how his skin doubled over itself. "Oh, my God, he looks like a giant turtle," I thought.

When we stopped for the night in Grants, New Mexico, Les wobbled into the lobby. I had to go back out to the SUV for his transport chair so that we could get him to the elevator and up to our room. He was too tired to go out for dinner, so Bob and Vicki picked up some sandwiches and ate with us.

The second day dawned cool, crisp, and full of sunshine. From I-40 we could see the red bluffs in the distance; gradually they recolored our mood.

Les and I had made this trip many times, but when we cut off at Holbrook to take the Beeline Highway into Mesa—over the Mogollon Rim, through Heber, into Payson—the majestic pines, the layers upon layers of blue-hued vistas, and the stately saguaros inspired us anew.

Les looked less shaky and tired. Maybe, just maybe, things would work out after all.

Keith, Kara, David, Kirsten, and Annika welcomed us with arms open wide. "We can't believe you're here."

For the next twelve days the family consoled and cared for us. They took us to see Ralph. We visited our favorite restaurants. They pushed Les in his chair as needed and found his cane when missing.

For the first time in months I did not lift a finger; I did not do everything that had to be done; I did not obsess over whether I should call the doctor or rush to the ER or just worry through the night. Les stabilized and seemed better each day.

The visits with Ralph, however, were grim. His stroke had dulled his eyes; his inability to carry on a meaningful conversation left us feeling empty. On the way home from one such visit I asked Les how he was doing.

"He looks like Ralph, but he doesn't seem like Ralph. I can barely stand it. He was always so active, so proud of his athleticism. We can't even talk sports or joke together."

It became clear that Les was not only seeing his brother weaken, but also feeling his own diminution. He said that he hated that he had lost so much stamina, that he was unable to help me as he would like, that he used a cane and sometimes had to be pushed in his transport chair. It was as if Ralph's incapacitation displayed a road map that frightened both of us.

But seeing Ralph had been part of our Bucket List and, sad as the visit had left us, we felt gratified that we had accomplished that.

The euphoric and final item on the BL, of course, was Kirsten's graduation. We had known all along that we wouldn't attend the ceremony. Les could not navigate the steps of a stadium and neither of us could sit on bleacher seats long enough for someone to intone over eight hundred names. We would simply revel in the party with the other grandparents and family.

In the meantime, two nights before graduation, we fashioned a crucial event for the two girls and us. We asked Kirsten whether she would mind sharing her graduation glory with her sister. Then we made sure that Annika understood and approved of this plan; she would not get another big gift next year.

I bought graduation cards and darling pink gift bags replete with orange tissue paper. Les wrote the checks. I slipped them into the cards that went into special little cosmetic zipper bags that went into the tissue paper that went into the bags. Pretty. Pretty.

We had supper with the girls at Chili's, our customary restaurant throughout their childhoods and teens. After the traditional baby ribs and shared molten chocolate cake, we presented the packages and requested that the girls open each part at exactly the same time.

The wide smiles on their faces, their unison "Oh, my! Oh, my!" and their floods of thanks became the highpoint of our whole trip. It was what we came to do. We did it.

You know that sensation when everything has turned out, when everything has fallen into place perfectly, when the stars have finally aligned?

That feeling of joy shimmered over our entire trip. It outshone our worries. Come what may, we got to Phoenix.

Back to Normal

"Hi! Welcome back. Come here, you two. Hugs and kisses, everyone. "

Karen and Emily reached out as we walked through our back door, while Bob and Vicki unloaded our luggage. Our white dishes and a vase of white tulips adorned the forest green cloth on the table. Chili bubbled on the stove. The six of us debriefed as we ate together.

Afterwards, while we drank our decaf and devoured the ubiquitous chocolates, Les announced, "I'm cured! I'm cured! It's a miracle. I'm cured."

Les' health *had* improved in Phoenix. The lower altitude helped his breathing. It also alleviated some of the fluid he had accumulated. He dropped a pound each day of the ten we were there, adding to the over thirty pounds lost during the previous year and a half. This man, who weighed 182 pounds most of his adult life, couldn't keep his jeans up.

But "I'm cured," he said.

And sometimes, indeed, it seemed as if he were. Dr. Smith even suggested that maybe we should go again in the fall and accept Keith's invitation to stay longer since it helped Les so much.

All summer, although his knee gave him fits, Les slogged around the yard pulling a weed here, digging a dandelion there. He began offering to do breakfast dishes. He'd say, "If you play piano for me, I'll do up the kitchen." No brainer. On Saturdays it was show tunes, on Sundays, hymns; the rest of the week I played Beethoven and Scott Joplin.

Slowly life returned to a semblance of normal. Certainly not the energetic, enthusiastic normal we had known, but tolerable. Certainly not as much active participation with our family, now numbering more than thirty persons and growing, but enough to be called Bapa and Ma.

However, with Les' knee continuing to deform, a replacement ever more out of the question, his cane not quite enough help, and a new brace not as supportive as we'd hoped, any sort of outing morphed into a hurdle. We kept Les' transport chair in the car for the times we arrived at a doctor's office and he was too tired to walk in. Or we went to a movie and the hall was too long.

A semblance of normal.

We weren't waving much, but we were swimming.

Parallel Universe

One warm evening in June Les and I had dinner with four friends from California. As we ate in a casual restaurant, sun slanting through the slatted blinds, basking in the pleasure of the unexpected visit, our conversation turned to places these late-sixty-somethings had visited in Denver that day.

"Have you been to the Botanic Gardens this year?" one asked. "They must be one of the top five in the country by now."

"Well, no," we said.

Actually we hadn't been there in the past five years. I murmured something about how hard it is for Les to get around; they assured us that they had seen many walkers and wheelchairs navigating the Gardens. I tried to explain that any visit would require my hoisting the transport chair into the backseat of our car and out again—both coming and going. Then I would need to push him over the asphalt, gravel, and stones.

Our friends leaned forward as their voices overlapped in persistence, "Hey, you look strong, Lois. You would both love it. Don't let this summer pass without going. The Gardens are beautiful. You mustn't miss them."

Later, after telling us about their upcoming weekend in Seattle, an impending German river cruise in the fall, and holiday plans in Brazil, one of them asked where *we'd* been recently. We mentioned our trip to Arizona.

And what big trips did we have coming up? I glanced at Les and saw the same incredulous expression on his face that I could feel spreading across mine. Our inability to be more adventurous began to feel quite inadequate.

I mumbled a few words about how we can't travel unless someone goes with us; our children graciously ferry us to visit family, but they are busy with their families and careers.

Our friends' puzzled expressions told us that they just didn't get it. They saw that we moved around our house reasonably well, that Les had walked into the restaurant with his cane, holding my arm. So why couldn't we just get in the car or hop on a plane? Could they have understood if I had told them that Les wasn't allowed to fly? He couldn't be at eight thousand feet for more than two or three hours, which essentially curtails most mountain excursions.

Would they have comprehended if I had explained that I was not up to driving long distances, that I would feel terrified to take Les far from home by myself? Earlier this year Les semi-collapsed in a McDonalds, just six miles from where we live. I had to ask a nice gentleman to help him to the bathroom. What would I do on the side of a road?

Should I have reminded our friends of my CFS? I have long since tired (pun intended) of explaining my chronic fatigue syndrome to others: How, by some evenings, I can't string words into a complete sentence. How, at a moment's notice, I can be unable to go one more step. How, if I don't pace myself, I have to take a day in bed to recuperate.

Our friends, of course, are years behind us. They think like we used to think.

They probably cannot grasp that if I were not eight years younger than Les, forcing myself to step up, he could well be in an assisted living facility, sitting in a wheelchair, eating institutional food. Many people in his age group, with his health and mobility problems, are in just such a place.

Do others note that we *do* live alone, handling our own affairs, and therefore they expect that we could accomplish all of the many things they can do?

Les and I see a wide chasm between being able to take care of ourselves in our home with its many grab bars and accommodations and being able to easily function, as we once did, in the larger world.

Sure, we can buy groceries and put them away, but we would not be able to pack a charcoal grill and drive into the mountains for a picnic. We can go to a movie, but could not walk into Coors Field and get seated at a Rockies' game. Certainly I can get us to our various appointments, but it would be bad judgment to drive out of town by ourselves. We do manage our lives, but the fact remains that we have made multiple adjustments and many concessions to our many infirmities.

Are Les and I more frustrated about our situation or by the fact that others are unable to understand it?

Seeing their expectations left us sad that we could not fulfill them and discouraged about even trying to explain the incomprehensible.

However, it would be unseemly and most ungrateful to think that persons coming up behind us are culpable or unkind for not yet being able to visualize old.

We are pleased that our family and friends see and treat us as capable, vital persons. It would not be an advantage to them—or us—if they could visualize our parallel universe.

And how can we possibly protest our longevity, and what accompanies it, when it feels so precious to be together?

Two Golden Peaches

T hree months later, two days before our sixty-sixth anniversary, I woke early. I remembered the fuzzy, juicy peaches in the basket on the counter that would be the best part of our breakfast today.

I reached to touch Les and listened to the patchy sound of his breathing.

As I rested beside him, I tried to think of something we could actually do to celebrate our day. Last year our children had hosted a weekend at a fancy downtown hotel, but sixty-six was not a Big Bash number. The BBs are only for fives and tens.

I would have liked to stay at Grand Lake Lodge, the site of our original honeymoon, but Les was not allowed to go to higher elevations; he certainly couldn't navigate the rugged path that led to the cabins. If he were having a good day, perhaps we could settle for a cozy dinner at the friendly Italian café just down the hill from home.

As I lay there in the dark, wishing I were asleep, oblivious to my world, thoughts raced through the murkiest corners of my mind.

For the past week or two I had been leafing through my 2013 diary, preparing to type up the summary page for *The Hjelmstad Story* scrapbook, continuing my life audit.

Someone once said that an unexamined life is not worth living, but sometimes I have to think that my examinations are ridiculous—seventy plus diaries, a summary page for each, an Excel page listing each of my six hundred and fifteen speeches, a whole file dedicated to health, lists of all the major things we have ever bought.

Does it really matter that we purchased our patio swing in 1979 or replaced our garbage disposal in years 1961, 1982, and 2001?

Nevertheless, rereading last year's diary was illuminating. I could see our struggle to stay in denial, to not waste a single day of our lives in a sea of apprehension. My goal was to turn off anticipatory grief. I mostly succeeded—except for early morning ruminations, nightly moments of dread, and those times when I caught myself looking at Les, overwhelmed by how much I love this man....

But I could also see how pushing down the fear sometimes crushed joy, too. I couldn't be selective in repressing emotions. When I willed away anxiety, my compassion also dissipated.

It was likewise in those pages that I saw how his heart problems and severe pulmonary hypertension had slowly but surely incapacitated Les. Often I had asked myself incredulously: How did he *suddenly* get old, *suddenly* lose more than forty pounds, *suddenly* become frail?

It had *not* been sudden. It was all right there in my diary—pound after pound, episode after episode, day after day. And in those pages I found myself scarcely breathing, holding on by my fingertips, falling into bed each night with a weariness that reached into my soul. Even my handwriting had deteriorated.

And *sudden* wasn't the word. Relentless, inexorable, inescapable maybe?

I shook off my musings, stretched, eased my aching joints out of bed, groaned into the kitchen, boiled some water, scalded and peeled those golden peaches, even more luscious than I had hoped.

Peaches in September radiate the waning warmth of summer, but the season never lasts.

All I can do is wait, love him more each day, and move forward, even while knowing that three lifetimes would not be enough.

Maybe We Have It Wrong

Before I began unpacking that late November evening after Les and I returned from Arizona, I listened to our many phone messages. The final call was from Gloria, the daughter of our friend Mel and his wife, the other Lois. The Lois who had been my bridesmaid and for whom I was matron of honor three months later. My lifelong friend Lois.

Gloria simply said, "Call my dad."

Keith had flown to Denver in early October to drive Vicki's SUV and the two of us down to Mesa, as Dr. Smith had suggested when our visit last May had proved to be so restorative. Bob and Vicki had flown to Mesa to bring us home. We had stayed in Arizona for six invigorating weeks.

Although we missed Denver's colorful Indian summer, being with Keith's family for that extended period had been recuperative. Knowing the parameters of our visit, Les and I quickly and easily settled into their routine. We made our own breakfast and lunch while Keith and Kara taught at ASU and the three kids were in various schools; we had dinner together and visited for an hour or so. When everyone went upstairs to do homework, make lesson plans, and grade papers, we retired to our own private quarters with its two big windows, easy chairs, TV, and computer.

It had been just what we needed—a touch mundane, but sufficient activity and companionship to almost lull us into thinking that we are not old, Les does not have health problems, our life has not changed. It offered him another opportunity to rest his body at the lower altitude and me a chance to reduce the concern that I feel so keenly at home.

But even in the lap of such a carefree existence and loving attention, thoughts of the time I may be alone intruded from the moment I awoke. No matter how much Les and I talked candidly and made coping plans for me, no matter how much we tried to live in the moment, thinking about the future often turned my insides into a tornado.

A bit of homesickness overtook us from time to time. By the end of six weeks, we were ready to come home. And here we were.

I took clean shirts and tops from our suitcases, shook out the wrinkles, and hung them in the closet. I told myself, "I'll return that call tomorrow. I'm much too tired tonight."

The next day tears were already spilling down my cheeks as I tapped in the numbers.

"Oh, Lois," Mel said immediately, no hello. "My Lois was just sitting in her chair reading when I ran out to pick up a loaf of bread. When I came back, she was, she was gone. She

was sitting in her chair…. She was just sitting in her chair….”
His sobs tore through the phone line.

I sat, dazed. My lifelong friend was dead. We had shared so much more than our weddings. We each had four children; her first was a daughter as was mine; their ages and the ages of our three sons are the same; we both had been very involved in our churches. We had never lived in the same state after our marriages, but when we visited one another we always took up exactly where we left off. I have sixty-some Christmas letters that tell the story of her life.

And so, another dear friend added to the host of lost loved ones. Another person who wasn't even sick just up and died. She was sitting in her chair. And she died.

I hunched over and covered my face with my hands.

I had been so confident that I couldn't die before Les. He's my responsibility, my barrier, my charm. While he is here I will be here: I need to care for him. I can't be sick; I can't have surgery for my bad back, break my arm, or even sprain my little finger. God wouldn't let that happen.

But the other Lois was not sick; she too was younger than her husband; he had health issues of his own and needed her. And I am eighty-four, for goodness' sake. Would it not be possible to just up and die? Even the idea disoriented me.

As I sat there in the bright sunshine, my mortality silently tiptoed up from behind, seized my throat, and gripped my heart.

Year 2015

The Yard

How will I manage the yard when you're gone?
How will I know when to aerate and water?
How will I keep cedar mulch from encroaching?
Fill all the pots without my dear potter?

Systems Fail

"Oh, no, Tony's left the practice?"

In early February that year, the day after my first sacroiliac joint injection, Les and I went to Dr. Porter's office for the regular pacemaker check. We were shocked to learn that the technician who had always worked with Les was gone. The temporary person was clueless. As our explanations of what needed to be done fell on deaf ears, our confidence crumbled.

Then we learned that Dr. Hanson, the man with whom we had navigated a number of cardiac crises, had walked into the office three weeks earlier, announced that he was done, burnt out, kaput, and walked back out.

Nine days later when I went in for follow-up, the spine doctor told me that it was his last day. His wife preferred to live in Florida and therefore he was moving tomorrow.

A couple of days later, I had a dental emergency, less than two hours before we were to leave for Arizona. Keith and Annika were flying in to drive us and our car back for our six-week spring visit.

When Les and I walked up to the receptionist's desk, we discovered that our dentist (the one who had replaced our longtime dentist last year) had moved to Boulder a month earlier. I would need to see a new dentist.

Four members of our health support team gone in two weeks and two days.

Oh, dear. Oh, dear. Over the years, each time we lost a trusted person, it unsettled us, wrenched us from our sense of comfort and security. Each time, we had stressed, found replacements, and gone on.

But four in two weeks?

Beauty All Around

"Are you ready to leave? Ready for a really fun road trip? Ready for R & R?" Keith asked as he and Annika walked through the back door an hour after the upsetting dental visit.

"Oh, yeah, more than ready," Les said.

The 843 miles passed quickly. We loved the forest around Santa Fe. I cracked my window to better enjoy the fresh smell of pine.

We had never gone to Arizona in February before. The full blooming of the desert astonished us—burgeoning trees and desert flowers spread in full splendor, white flowers embellishing the tops of the saguaros, and ever-present paloverde shimmering in lacy yellow dress.

And in Mesa, the spring glory continued. It had rained a lot; the Texas sage was arrayed in dazzling purple; the bougainvillea flourished brilliant red.

We found it both convenient and pleasurable to have our car with us. We could duck out for a quick lunch, pick up a prescription at Walgreens, or drive down Power Road to the movie theater at Superstition Springs. Power Road was lined with oleander and fruit trees heavy with white, pink, and red blossoms.

Once, as we returned to our car after a brief visit to the mall, a woman stopped us in the parking lot and said, "I don't mean to intrude, I'm sorry, uh, but you two are the most adorable couple I have ever seen. I just had to tell you."

Most afternoons I worked at the desk in our suite, gazing out the large south window, admiring the lavender fairy dusters, yellow lantana, and spiky agave. I typed, cut, pasted, and revised.

Sometimes I shed a tear or two as I reminisced, as I tried to wrap my head around the world in which Les and I had lived since he turned ninety. Was I writing about aging, about love? Was I writing to remember—or forget? It was hard work. I needed the occasional distraction provided by small lizards skittering across the front patio.

Our visits with Ralph were even grimmer than they had been last fall. His vascular dementia had worsened. Only once did he know us. He opened his eyes and slurred, "Oh, hi, Lesh. You, too, Loish."

The last time we visited, Les asked him a simple question. Ralph started to mumble a word or two, then fixed his eyes above the TV as if his answer somehow lay there. If only….

Les held my arm and leaned on his cane as we crunched on the gravel driveway back to our car.

He turned toward me and said, "I have lost my brother. Dear Ralph Waldo is gone…."

I put my arms around him and held him close. Then Kara drove us home through canopies of amazing color.

But the pervasive beauty surrounding us did not cancel the perplexity that my writing prompted or halt Ralph's unyielding deterioration.

Meltdown

Back home, several days before Les turned ninety-three, he limped into the kitchen, "I don't feel at all well today. My knee is killing me. My head feels fuzzy. Yuck."

It was Saturday, so I made eggs and pancakes for breakfast. That boosted him a bit, but once we had each inquired about how the other had slept and he had complimented me on the "perfecto eggs," the conversation died. It was clear that Les not only felt unwell but depressed.

We cleaned up the kitchen and read the paper. Les decided to try the topical knee-pain medicine Dr. Smith had recently prescribed for him.

He read the *Warnings and Cautions and Side Effects* paper and, as usual, flipped out. After a person has read one of those warnings, it's a miracle anyone is compliant with any medication. He sat in his chair looking morose, and applied a dab of the expensive cream to his offending joint.

"It isn't helping," he said. "Nothing helps."

Les had planned to hose off the patio before noon so he grabbed his walker and staggered out to the garage to find the brass nozzle. Then he looked in the tool shed.

"I can't find it anywhere," he grumbled, "I know it was here last time I looked. Somebody hid it. Can't find anything in my garage. And half the stuff is gone after you and Russ cleaned it out last fall."

"I'll look for you," I said.

But the nozzle was nowhere to be found. Les tried to push his walker in the grass. He became more and more frustrated.

"I'm so clumsy. If only I could get around like I did before."

"I know, sweetheart, I know."

Off we went to the hardware store to buy another nozzle. Again almost unable to walk, Les gripped a cart to steady himself. The greeter looked puzzled. I mentioned how difficult it is for him to walk.

She whispered to me, "Even through his jeans, that knee looks awfully swollen."

"He's going to be ninety-three on Monday," I offered, thinking she'd be surprised and amazed that he looked so good for his age. Everyone said that.

"Well, my mom is ninety-six and she gets around just fine."

Oh, great. Goody for her.

I found the nozzle and did not engage in any more small talk with clerks.

When we got home, I helped Les clean the patio. Actually, he sat in a chair and watched. I used the new nozzle to wet the surface, scrubbed away the dark stains from last autumn's leaves, rinsed. The hose snaked away from me, soaking my T-shirt and jeans. I stood there, dripping wet and freezing cold.

Les said, "I absolutely *hate* that you have to do all of this stuff."

In the afternoon I worked on our finances while Les matched receipts to the credit card statements. There were bills, stubs, and papers everywhere. When I tried to reconcile the statement on QuickBooks, I was off by thousands of dollars. Again, frustration reigned.

By the time we had dinner and looked for a movie to watch, our moods had sunk lower than a snail to the ground. We were both exhausted. We ached. We didn't want to watch the same movie. He liked "true." I needed "easy."

Finally I huffed, "I'm going downstairs to my office to figure out my numbers problem. You just do whatever the hell you wish."

An hour and a half later, having solved the QuickBooks discrepancy, I came up to our bedroom where Les sat.

We undressed in silence. Then Les couldn't locate his pajama top. He had put it in the wrong drawer, but I found it and handed it to him.

"No, not this one. I want that softer one with the shorter sleeves that I always wear."

"This is that one," I said.

"No, it's not."

"It's the same one you've worn for four years."

"No, it is not."

"It's the one you wore while we visited Keith's."

"No. It. Is. Not."

"It is. It is," I yelled.

"You're mean," he said.

I started to cry.

And then I melted down. I wept. I wailed. I sobbed until my body shook so much that I collapsed onto the bed.

Les came and sat beside me, "I'm sorry. I didn't mean to make you cry."

He stroked my hair. He patted my hand. He lay down on the bed, rolled toward me, and put his arm over me.

"Sweetheart, I apologize. I can't stand to see you cry like this."

Between my sputters I managed to say, "It's not your fault."

I was like a two-year-old, kicking and screaming on the floor, who doesn't know what she wants, but is quite certain that this isn't it.

Les held me a long time and, although my eyes were damp the rest of the evening, I calmed down to the point where we could examine the meltdown.

No, it hadn't been a stellar day. And yes, we had a little spat, but we've had a lot of spats, some with a great deal more content. Certainly this one should not have caused that earthquake. What happened?

Gradually we realized that while we had been with Keith and Kara, we were able to stay in quasi-denial. We had a great road trip; it seemed as if we were on vacation; other people surrounded us daily, keeping us on our best behavior, distracting us. We had tailored our feelings to meet their expectations of their guests.

But on this particular Saturday—watching Les try so hard to do what needed doing; seeing how fragile we were in trying to stay in and manage our home; hearing Les deny over and over that the pajama top he'd used as recently as six days ago was his—our ages of eighty-four and almost ninety-three fell on us like a blanket of lead.

Our golden years had long since tarnished.

My therapist had once told me, "Compared to senescence, adolescence is a walk in the park."

We wept for what has been, what is, and what will be.

Priceless

Rain pelted the roof all night. When we opened the shutters, the world looked damp and sodden. Our pine trees dripped. However, I was determined to make a special ninety-third birthday for Les.

Pancakes and eggs, oh yes. Love in the morning, check. Special present? A rough draft of this book. The messy sheaf of papers thrilled him.

We leisurely read the paper. I didn't ask if he wanted to go see a movie since his usual reply is "Today? I don't think so." I simply suggested that he shave, shower, dab on the Jovan Musk cologne that I love, then go out to the car.

The theater had recently installed lounger seats, so it was a pleasure to watch *While We're Young*, a movie in which Ben Stiller tried to recreate his twenties and got conned instead. The movie portrayed the lead characters as old. Old? They were in their *forties*.

After the show, we caught an early dinner before I took Les for the last surprise.

He had been using his cane for over a year. We had the simple transport chair that we used when he was too ill to walk, but what he really needed was a rollator—a wheelchair-like contraption that could be used as a walker or a wheelchair. One that had a seat where he could sit to rest plus a basket to carry things. One in which, with a minor adjustment, I could push him when needed. One that enabled him to walk more quickly and with less strain than the cane did.

It was 5:17 when we finished dinner; the medical supply store closed at 5:30. I concentrated on driving safely, but wasted no time. The two saleswomen could not get over "How cute you are; what an adorable old couple," but they found the exact equipment we required and taught us how to use it. Every day for weeks after that Les told me that it was the best present he had ever received.

When someone can be excited over a rollator, birthdays are easily made priceless.

Harbor

Throughout these many years
each time you took my hand in yours
the seas of life calmed and settled

And even now when that weathered hand
reaches for mine
I feel as if I have sailed rough seas
and just entered my harbor

In-valid

Ralph died in June, two months after our last visit. Bob and Vicki offered to take us to his service. We left on a Thursday, planning to drive two days, stay in Mesa two days, and return home on Monday and Tuesday.

The funeral was on Saturday. Although it was 109° outside, the sanctuary of Resurrection Lutheran Church in Scottsdale was cool and dim. Organ music played softly. The mourners sat quietly.

Ralph's three daughters had asked me to read a piece I had written and, although my voice faltered a bit, I was able to get through the tribute to the man whose wife had been my best friend, to the brother-in-law I dearly loved.

I offered some memories—how, when they were young, Les and Ralph drew football fields on paper and moved a navy bean around to show where the ball was as they listened to games on the radio; how Les left high school as Ralph entered; how for decades Ralph and Mary Jo had been the couple with whom we played, shared advice, and commiserated.

Ralph's death truly ended the era of bringing up our families, retiring, and facing old age together. Les and I would feel the losses of our dear friends for the rest of our lives.

The girls wrote afterwards: *You and your family coming all that way to be with us turned a day that was very hard into a time of sharing memories that we will treasure forever.* Making the trip was clearly the right thing to do.

Sunday I awoke with a fever of almost 103°. I could barely raise my head. When we left for home on Monday I lay back, sat motionless, and only got in and out of the car with help. By the time we got home Tuesday night, I fell into bed, rumpled travel clothes and all.

Wednesday I took Les to his routine visit with Dr. Smith. The doctor heard my cough, listened to my chest, and said, "Whoa! Whoa, my dear! You have pneumonia!" He listened some more. "It's really a good thing you came in today." He sent me home with a strong antibiotic and the strict admonition, "I know you need to stay with Les, but if anything changes, *anything at all*, go directly to the hospital."

The pneumonia knocked me for a loop. Actually, as I cope with CFS, most anything knocks me for a loop. My weakness lasted so long, I wasn't sure I'd ever get back to my baseline. Les had maintained most of his strength and stamina until he was ninety. Was eighty-four my expiration date?

I felt invalid, in-valid. As though I wasn't a person anymore. Like I couldn't fight my way out of a paper bag, to use a terrible cliché. Why would one be in a paper bag, anyway?

I had long concluded that dying first was my main worry. But I now realized how perilous our life could become if I became sicker and frailer.

The biggie, of course, is the inevitability of our goodbyes— a thing without feathers; hope can stretch only so far.

First Kiss Remembered

The middle of July, as I straightened the appliquéd quilt on our queen bed, still weak from the pneumonia, I called out, "Happy anniversary, darling." It pleased me that we could celebrate something good after many months of dealing with illness and related tests.

"What?" Les said. We always say what. It gives us a moment to replay what the other person said, to process the words for meaning, to think of an appropriate response or any response at all for that matter.

"Happy anniversary!"

He looked puzzled and paused to think. "Oh, yeah, July 13. The anniversary of our first kiss. And that's how many years?"

"Sixty-eight."

Anything could happen in sixty-eight years and many things had. We had been together almost 25,000 days—routine, repetitive, ecstatic, downright horrific days.

I put our coffee, toast, and eggs on a tray and carried it out to the sturdy deck which, years earlier, Les had built without a blueprint or plan. The garden of tea roses offered a vision of tiny white and red flowers; the hanging baskets swayed gently in a slight breeze; the aspen leaves quaked as intended. A profusion of lavender, purple, and coral petunias spilled out of their bowls, their fragrance filling the air around us.

"It would be fun to get out the old diaries again," Les said, as he wiped his lips with his napkin.

I dashed downstairs to my stash of seventy volumes to get 1946, 1947, and 1948. The pages were yellowed and brittle— we have revisited our courtship many times—but legible. I read various passages to him and together we refashioned our story:

We met on Thanksgiving Day 1946. A week earlier my mother had announced, "We're going to have Thanksgiving with Harold and Doris." I didn't want to eat with my parents' friends from church or play with their little girls, but I went.

I don't recall who said what during the lively conversation. I assume I talked because I always did, but Harold's visiting twenty-four-year-old brother was quiet. Recently discharged from the Navy, Les was a handsome man—tall, deep blue eyes, blond, unusually tan for November. After dessert, he pushed away from the table and leaned back in his chair, his hands clasped behind his head, his beautiful long legs stretched out…. Oh, my.

Les found a job and stayed in Denver. Throughout the winter, he occasionally smiled at me at church. By March I had broken up with the last of a long string of boyfriends.

In June Les gave me a ride home from Youth Group. When I turned to thank him, he drew me close. We sat in silence a long time before I finally ran into the house. I felt sheltered, secure in his arms.

Then my family and I left on a two-week vacation. We'd been home a week when Les called, "Could we go bowling tonight?"

"Tonight? I have to shampoo my hair tonight."

"Please? Please?"

I had never bowled before that evening. I never have since.

Three days after that Les took me home from choir practice. As we sat in front of my house he told me that he loved me. I didn't believe him. It was way too soon.

Two days later, we went to the mountains with Harold and Doris for a picnic. On the way home, he said it again, and for some reason I starting believing him. Two days and now it's not too soon?

And three days after that, on July 13, 1947, Les kissed me. I had never been kissed before. I snuggled my face next to his, almost drowning in the tenderness of his lips and the subtle scent of his aftershave as he kissed me again and again.

I am going to marry this guy....

Now, when I look back at that slender young girl with her long dark hair, green eyes, appealing mouth, and quite attractive breasts, I marvel at her innocence—and her sureness. Even though she was the oldest of three siblings, even though she was mature for her age, she was a child. She could not have possibly known what a marriage might be, given that she knew no good role models. Where was her caution, her fear?

But Les had kissed her. The chemistry was immediate, intense, and, inarguably, enduring.

The sun was high overhead before Les finally said, "Oh, wow! I adore this story, but who would have thought we'd be out here this long? Let's go in. It's too warm."

I picked up the diaries. We went into the house to make love.

And now, even in the midst of grueling uncertainty and uneven recovery, the two of us can relive this story and revel in the long years it presaged. We can bring to mind how crazy-in-love we were. We reference it when we are exceedingly happy and when things become dicey. It serves as a resource in our marriage—a way to remember why we married in the first place.

It is our talisman. It is our grace.

OK, OK, We Looked

The first week of September, as I walked into the lobby of a retirement center, I muttered to myself, "I don't want to do this; I really can't be here; I'm too exhausted to cope."

I had just driven by the main building twice. Then when I dropped Les off at the front door, I couldn't find a parking place—even though there were four spaces reserved near the entrance with names on them and one plainly said MR. and MRS. LES HJELMSTAD.

Molly welcomed us at the Sales Desk so enthusiastically and complimented us so thoroughly on "What an adorable couple you are," that I turned around to look. I mean, apparently we are cute, but really. We do not understand our oft-noted adorableness, but her welcome did soften my frowning face to some extent.

Earlier that week, Les and I had decided that maybe we should rethink our ongoing default position of "carry us out of our house feet first." My pneumonia and slow recovery had been disconcerting. Our friends, family, and AARP had long since asked why we hadn't moved to a retirement center.

In fact, about ten years ago, we had looked intensively at a dozen or so facilities. I dutifully took notes, garnered blueprints, and mentally moved furniture. Perhaps, someday, when we were old.

Of course, all of the places we had visited previously kept us updated over the years. Many brochures. Many emails. Many phone calls. We always said not yet. But we had kept a couple of possibilities in mind. Six of our friends had recently moved to Wind Crest.

Now there we were with sweet Molly. She even had a wheelchair for Les.

We visited the appropriate apartments and again I mentally arranged objects, puzzling, "Where will I put my Christmas trees? I can leave most of my stuff behind, but not Christmas!"

I thought about the ruby red glasses and the Curiosity Shop dinner plates that we had acquired in antique malls across the country. The cupboards didn't look very big. I couldn't imagine not entertaining anymore.

"Where will my two St. Francis of Assisi statues stand? And which wall will hold my piano? Leaving my piano behind is a deal-breaker."

Two long hours, many long halls, and one too many friendly hellos later, Les and I dragged our exhausted selves out to the car. He had been so enthusiastic about making this visit and so interested in all the amenities that I feared my reservations and misgivings were one-sided. Not so.

When we weighed the pros and cons, we thought that maybe it could be harder to manage living there than it is at home. Now, we can navigate the main floor easily. Our garage is right next to the kitchen. Our car is in that garage. At Wind Crest Les would need to walk with his rollator—or sit in it while I pushed him—to traverse the endless halls.

We evaluated the amazing amenities Molly had listed: pool, gym, gourmet restaurants, new friends, parking space for a fee, EMTs.

However, neither of us swims; we have exercise equipment at home; we are too tired in the evening to go out to eat; we already have friends and family for whom we barely have time and energy; we have a free garage only two steps from our kitchen; we can unload groceries on the same two steps.

Granted, Wind Crest offers an impressive variety of clubs, but Les is an introvert like me. With my monthly Writers' Group, frequent breakfasts with my siblings, and our children stopping by, we have enough interaction. If we have an emergency we live four blocks from one hospital and eight from another. An ambulance could be here faster than I could remove my nail polish and reapply.

But the one service we most needed, housekeeping, was not offered. When I inquired, Molly told us that, yes, we could hire someone to come in. Same thing for assisted living. And when the time arrived, we would need to call the Denver Metro Hospice.

Duh.

We figured we could employ assistance at home. Hospice would undoubtedly come to our house, too.

We didn't close our minds to getting on a priority list, but we decided that we'd wait to move until we actually get old. And there was always that "carry me out feet first."

As for housekeeping—

Cleanliness Is Next to Godliness

When I was a small girl, I often played house, putting play dishes in the tiny cupboard my father had made, baking pretend cakes in the little oven, pushing my wee broom, and wielding my tiny wool duster unendingly....

As a teen bride, I tried to make a home out of our ramshackle old farmhouse: continually wiping up coal dust; sewing fresh, crisp polka dot curtains; and arranging the dilapidated furniture into a configuration that I did not yet know was feng shui.

The first house we owned was a mere 600 square feet; we had almost no furniture. But because I learned homemaking from my impeccable mother and because the 1950s mantra was "Cleanliness Is Next to Godliness," I washed the woodwork every Friday whether it needed it or not.

Our second house was 840 square feet with a full basement. It took a bit longer to clean, but I was in my twenties; it hardly fazed me. I called Mondays, Wednesdays, and Fridays "Demon Days" and swished through the house.

We moved into our third and current house the year after our fourth child was born. It is only 1250 square feet on the main floor, but at that time it had three bedrooms plus a full basement half-finished with a twelve by twenty-four foot playroom and a big "Futility" Room. Les helped me clean when he wasn't working overtime.

As our lives evolved, so did the house. It seemed roomy enough when the kids were small. They shared bedrooms until Les completed two more in the basement. They built tiny villages on the oval braided rug in the playroom.

When I began teaching piano, the big room morphed into a music studio. Even as the kids grew into teenagers, the house accommodated the six of us fairly well. It became more difficult to keep it anywhere near immaculate, but the kids were strong; everyone had chores. I turned a deaf ear to the grumbling.

Now, sixty years later, the house fits Les and me well—the two basement bedrooms turned into private offices, two of the upstairs bedrooms combined into a large master, the other changed into a den, and the studio revamped into an exercise room.

But it still gets gritty. Not as often and not as quickly, but gritty. And I still want it shipshape.

After Les retired more than twenty-five years ago, and certainly after my CFS and breast cancer began two years later, he voluntarily took over some of the heavier housework. When he became ill, Vicki helped us for a year or so until her own health problems sidetracked her. Karen and Emily also filled in.

But when Les had regained a bit more energy last spring and summer, we wanted to reassert our independence. "We can do it ourselves," we said, our voices full of more hope than was warranted.

We tried. Les teetered around with his cane and a long-handled duster while I whooshed over the floors, but we got too tired. Since neither of us could manage the vacuum, the house was not clean enough to qualify for any sort of piety.

I researched intensively online and queried anyone who came within an ear's reach in an effort to find help. After gathering copious information I called a number of individuals and companies, then interviewed a person who checked out well.

And in a perfect placement of the planets, our soon-to-be-beloved Tiana and Dimitri came to our house the very afternoon following our visit to Wind Crest. After a veritable whirlwind of vigor and dedication, not even I could detect a speck of dust anywhere. They cleaned the inside of the microwave and toaster oven, washed the baseboards, climbed up to dust everything on the soffit, wiped the walls and into every corner....

Sacrificing our independence in the area of cleanliness, if not Godliness, allowed us to keep our independence on the much larger scale of staying in our home and guiding our lives.

The Leaves Turned

Twenty days later, we drove north on Downing Street, past Washington Park, enchanted by the overhang of leaves turning gold and red, eager for our biweekly visit with Dr. Smith.

He was the doctor who had managed Les' health, or lack thereof, through the past several years. He was the one who asked the right questions, prodded his colleagues, and listened to our every word. He had become the linchpin of our medical team. He was our cheerleader, our optimist, our "You aren't ready for hospice" guy.

We had seen him every other week for the past three years. He wanted to identify subtle changes and deal with them before they became major problems. And it had worked. Les still dealt with his damaged heart, serious pulmonary hypertension, and painful knee, but he was stable. Our lives were tumbling forward.

We knew Dr. Smith well and loved him equally well. He had heard what we said about heroic measures and quality of life issues. He had promised to support us in these concerns. Together we had formed an important partnership. He got us.

We pulled up to the building. Les heaved himself out of the car and walked in while I parked. The visit was routine. Dr. Smith inquired about Les' current health, read his daily weight chart, took his blood pressure, listened to his lungs, and signaled a thumbs-up.

Then he drew his wheelie chair close and quietly said, "I have to talk with you two about something." I tensed. Les leaned forward.

"I'm leaving this practice."

Les and I gasped in unison.

"As you know, my boys are six and ten. My wife needs my help and I just have to spend more time with them before they're gone." Les and I knew how that went. It would happen in the blink of an eye.

Dr. Smith went on to tell us that he had found a job as Medical Director of a company working to improve life for those in nursing homes.

We couldn't disagree with either reason nor did we. We told him we supported him fully. But our eyes filled with tears. His misted a bit, too. He explained that we would see Dr. Nelson, a new doctor whom he had personally trained. We expressed appreciation for his providing ongoing care.

But Dr. Smith? Our dear Dr. Smith was leaving?

My mind harkened back to February when—in the course of two weeks and two days—two physicians, one technician, and one dentist disappeared from our lives. It had seemed nearly catastrophic, especially since, as elderly patients with Medicare, we would not be accepted into many practices. It had been hard to find new helpers.

Dr. Smith could not be replaced.

In all our years of medical issues and an endless string of physicians of various specialties, he had been our best fit;

the one we had expected would easily outlive us; the one who would guide us through final days.

We drove home south on Downing Street. The sun had hidden behind a cloud. The leaves had dulled to brown.

The Age of Old-Old

Just days after that, on my eighty-fifth birthday, I finished my chores and sat down in the Windsor rocker to enjoy a cup of raspberry tea. Our kids had hosted my second Big Bash the previous weekend. Now I wanted to privately honor my day.

As I rocked back and forth I remembered my father once saying that 65-75 is Young-Old and 75-85 is Middle-Old. Eighty-five and up is simply Old-Old.

I wanted to mark my entry into such a momentous section of life in two ways: by reflecting back to my eightieth year when I was in the middle of *Middle-Old* and by rereading *This Path We Share.*

The reflection came first:

This Path was published the year I turned eighty. I had worked on it for twelve years. When the two thousand copies arrived, Les listened attentively as I recounted some of the steps I had taken to finally finish it—classes at Lighthouse Writers Workshop where I met my cherished Writers' Group; three readings by a content editor; two readings by a copy editor; many meetings with my cover designer.

When I woke up on my birthday I was happy about the book and thrilled to have made it. (I had superstitiously feared that I might not reach eighty.) It was also the first time I had been eligible for one of the Big Bashes. What could be in store? My dear husband had not made a career of event planning.

Around noon Les told me to pack a small bag and be ready at three-thirty. At 3:29 he took our bag and put it in the car. I stood in the garage, hands on my hips, and laughed, "Okay. But where is the limo?"

The doorbell rang. Karen, Bob, and Vicki presented me with a beautiful corsage. And parked at the curb was a long, black limo. I climbed in. From the back seat Keith and Russ said in unison, "Well, hello, Mother."

We hurried off to downtown Denver for an extraordinary weekend—fancy dinners, a concert, long strolls on the Sixteenth Street Mall. Big Bashes are always sensational.

But stepping over the brink into my eighties felt like entering another world; I did a lot of thinking during that entire year.

I did not like turning fifty—darn bifocals and orthopedic shoes. Then when I was fifty-eight, my ongoing battle with CFS began. My breast cancer diagnosis twenty-three years ago, first mastectomy, and radiation therapy marred my fifty-ninth year. I was more than happy to turn sixty, glad to be alive.

And seven is such a beautiful number that I loved the seventies. Seventy-one, seventy-three, seventy-seven....

But eighty? It seemed different. It looked different. Maybe the sixties are the new forties. Maybe the seventies are the new fifties. But the eighties are just the eighties.

Erik Erickson, a well-known psychoanalyst, has written that the task of old age is integration. Old age is a time to think back on life, assess what we may have contributed, own our gifts, face our regrets, deal with our many losses, and finally decide who we want to be when we grow up.

Publishing my third book, the story of our marriage, in the same year as I turned eighty brought it all full circle. I had completed my life audit in time to cross that threshold.

It had been fun remembering my eightieth year and that birthday, but I also wanted to allow myself the luxury of rereading all of *This Path* in one sitting and now it was time.

I put away my teacup, opened the book, and began. Midmorning turned to noon. The sun came around to the west window of the living room. I continued to read.

As I turned page after page, astonishment fell over me. From the vantage point of my additional five years I could see that the thousands of hours I spent writing our marriage story ended up doing more than I had envisioned—the book not only narrated our lives, but also assimilated them.

My reading showed that somehow Les and I had made our lives stand for something. We would not one day die without having truly lived. I could see in those many lines how crises had motivated us, how challenge had taught us, and how courage had become our partner.

That October afternoon as I commenced my eighty-sixth year, I celebrated our past with all its sorrow and joy and launched my Age of Old-Old.

A Foreign Land

The Saturday before Thanksgiving, Bob and Vicki picked us up to go spend the holiday with our youngest son, Russ, in Traverse City, Michigan. We had not imagined we could ever go back.

As we drove northeast from Denver on I-76, the sun peeked over the horizon in an inspiring blaze of red. And as it climbed higher, thousands of tiny diamonds sparkled on each tree branch. Steam rose from the riverbed and all the vegetation was etched in white frost.

Unfortunately the road was covered with black ice. We counted at least fifty vehicles strewn about like toys across a living room floor—cars in the ditch, pickups caught on guardrails, semi-trucks lying helplessly on their sides.

As we merged onto I-80 in Nebraska, the iciness, wreckage, and sunshine gave way to a vast, empty quietness of gray. I was struck by the absence. If we were to call to the heavens, would anyone answer? The dismal late autumnal skies continued through the entire thirteen-hundred miles. I occasionally rested my head against the window and thought about our many previous trips to Michigan, the helping with projects, the darling grandchildren.

I remembered a time when our grandson Robert, then age four, and Les had been going out to walk.

"It's gonna be a hike," Robert had said, as Les helped him into his jacket.

"Can't we just walk?"

"No, Bapa, it's not a walk, it's a *hike*."

After they had gone past the row of pine trees that edged the property, Robert stopped in his tracks, looked up at Les with his own set of big blue eyes, and said, "We have to make fond memories with our grandparents." They trekked on.

Suddenly Robert had stopped again and wistfully asked, "How do you make fond memories?"

Now Robert was twenty-six and waiting when we pulled up to his father's home.

As we were driving up Peninsula Drive to the house, I panicked a time or two, flashing back to the last time we were there, three years past—the day that Russ drove us to the airport in Grand Rapids, the day that Les subsequently collapsed in DIA.

We had made this trip so many times that I recognized most of the houses nestled against the hillside across from Grand Traverse Bay, but something seemed alien, unfamiliar.

By Wednesday, twelve of us had gathered, even Robert's girlfriend, Jessica, and Lyndsey's boyfriend, Matt. Never mind that more than twenty members of our immediate family could not make this get-together. Twelve was a substantially good round number.

During our five-day stay we were treated to a profusion of delicious food, much animated discussion, loud bursts of laughter, three gentle snowfalls, and a number of thoughtful one-on-one conversations.

But sometimes, amidst all the jolliness and fun, Les and I felt disoriented. We knew these people and loved them very much, but why did everything feel so different? Why did it seem as if we inhabited a parallel universe, a far-off land, a place where we did not understand the language?

The conversations were too swift to process, the overlapping voices too loud to hear. The discussions flowed so quickly that we saw few opportunities to jump in and swim along. There was no way I could make myself heard. Perhaps if I had a microphone, a megaphone, a bullhorn?

Every meal Russ sat in his arm chair at one end of the long wide table. Les and I sat together on a piano bench at the other end. We had been offered chairs. We had been commanded to sit in chairs. But we needed to sit close so I could whisper in his ear, rub his back, and reassure him. So he could put his arm around me or reach for my hand. We needed to be together on that bench to feel coupled.

We recognized that it was important that we be at this mini-reunion. We are the cornerstones of this family, clearly loved, the patriarch and matriarch. Maybe our presence even offered a barrier between our children and their mortality.

But we were also invisible.

We sat at the periphery of our family. Les frequently asked, "What did he say?" "Why is everyone laughing?" "Did I miss another joke?" Sometimes I could fill him in; sometimes I hadn't understood, either.

Due to our advanced ages we were allowed, nay urged, to retire at nine each evening. We left the cacophony behind and snuggled together to regroup, regain our sense of self, and renew our strength.

And as the days went on, we began to understand. Les and I were the foreigners. We had moved to a country that our family had not yet visited. We spoke their language, but they did not know ours.

I well remembered how I viewed elderly persons when I was younger—they sat quietly in the background, wizened and worn, speaking little. I supposed that they were used to being old and didn't mind. I did not see, nor was I interested in, the many years they had lived. I did not speculate how their lives had been or what they may have experienced to earn those sparse gray hairs and the creases furrowing their sad faces.

I do not know how it is for other people, but Les and I feel that living in the Land of Old Age is surreal. We are surprised to be here, unable to conceive of how we got here this quickly. The infirmities and inabilities of our bodies astonish us. The images in the mirror startle.

One afternoon as I rested, I pondered the dichotomy of our visit—we were making tender memories even in our disorientation, even as our equilibrium wobbled. Four generations were sharing a major holiday, all in different stages of life. We carried within us all the ages we have ever been. We remembered being the ages that each of them were, but no one could remember ours. Could we connect? How?

The Thanksgiving dinner table was set beautifully—the gold-trimmed crystal goblets shone; the tall candles glowed;

the burnished reds, rusts, and oranges of the fall centerpiece lent a festive tone. Russ asked each of us in turn to share something for which we were grateful. The responses softened our hearts and caused a wet cheek or two.

All the comments were poignant, of course, but Jessica touched us most powerfully as she expressed her love and appreciation for Robert. She said that without his support she would not have made it through the past rough year as she completed her doctorate. She spoke of her joy in being there with his family, "Each of you has made me so welcome. I almost feel as if I am part of you."

Then it was Robert's turn. Playing off her remarks, he talked about how important family was to him, how much we all had meant to him over the years. The fond memories had been made.

Then he fumbled in the pocket of his sport coat. Jessica's hand flew over her mouth as Robert knelt down, "Jessica, you should not only *feel* part of this family, you should *be* part of our family. Will you marry me?" She screamed, "Yes, yes, yes!" then cried as they kissed.

There were tears in everyone's eyes as we held hands across the generations. I could tell by the way that Matt looked at Lyndsey that they would be next. We began our Thanksgiving meal by chanting our family childhood prayer: *God is great, God is good.*

At that moment, Les and I didn't care whether we'd heard anything else all week. We felt included once again.

This family began in our love and remains rooted in that love, in our integrity, and in our faithfulness. This family will go on when Les and I exit the Land of Old Age and enter into Whatever-is-next.

The countryside seemed unreal; the landscape was foreign. But Gratitude folded us into her arms and held us tightly.

In the Bleak Midwinter

"Blood. There's blood in my urine."

I stirred from a heavy sleep.

The red, green, and blue lights of Christmas outlined our roof, sparkled through the window above our bed, and transformed the room into an authentic holiday wonderland. But Les was bellowing from the bathroom.

"Blood. There's a lot of blood."

There was indeed blood. Bright red.

I called the doctor. He asked me to bring Les down to the office for a urine test. The next day he called back, "There is significant blood in the sample. You need to see your urologist."

Feeling this to be an urgent turn of events, I fussed as much as I needed in order to get an appointment as soon as possible, which was five days hence. A major blizzard descended on that day. The receptionist tried to reschedule for two weeks later. Again I persisted, gently I hoped, and we got into the urologist's office the next afternoon. By then there was no more blood, so we could not help but consider the visit a fool's errand.

Our regular urologist wasn't in; we saw a new fellow whom we liked immediately. He said that the protocol for bladder bleeding was a CT and a cystoscopy. He looked aghast when Les asked how soon we could resume sex after a cystoscopy, his younger-than-springtime professionalism slipping for the briefest of moments.

The very thoughtful doctor quickly checked his watch and offered to try to get both tests done before we went home.

By then the sun was lowering in the sky and I began to worry about driving on the icy roads. However, I was so concerned about Les that I dropped that minor worry into a mental wastebasket filled with other unserviceable angst.

The nurse prepped Les for the cystoscopy. By now neither he nor I cared if his penis was out there for the world to see— I had seen it before, the nurse had seen thousands. I settled in to watch the procedure on the screen. Fascinating pictures. Nice smooth bladder, nice smooth bladder, smooth bladder.

The doctor, Les, and I saw it simultaneously. A big, ugly, ragged-edged tumor.

"There it is," the doctor said.

"Oh, my God," I said.

Les just stared.

"Bladder cancer. I'm hoping it's noninvasive, but we'll need to get that out."

This was serious. I could not be overcome with emotion. I needed to be proactive, raise questions:

"What are the chances it is benign?" I asked.

"I've seen a lot of these. Trust me, it's not benign."

"What will happen if we do nothing?"

"It will kill him in a year or two."

"What if it is invasive?"

"There won't be anything to do. We can't do the remove-the-bladder-make-another-opening procedure on someone almost ninety-four."

An aide scuttled Les over to another area for his CT scan and directed me to that waiting room. I found it, sank into a brown armchair, and wound my arms tightly around my trembling torso.

I looked west through the huge plate glass window and watched the silhouette of the Rocky Mountains disappear into darkness.

Year 2016

Let them nibble
Let them nibble
Let them nibble

These fears of not knowing
these fears of knowing
these fears of not being ready
not able to cope
not prepared to go on

Let them nibble on my heartstrings
Let them nibble in the corners of my mind
Let them nibble at the essence of my soul

Let them not consume our love

Happy New Year

Surgery was scheduled for January 15. We were guardedly optimistic about the actual procedure, but again most concerned about the anesthesia. The doctor reassured us. Sort of. Everything will be okay. Again, until it's not.

Les and I busied ourselves with cataloguing the Christmas cards and gifts, reorganizing the house after five major holiday events, taking down decorations, getting pre-op clearance, and updating our medical powers of attorney. The days crept by.

Friday the fifteenth, we got up at 4:15 a.m. We had preplanned our clothes, because we don't function well in the wee hours. Karen and Emily had stayed overnight so that they could take us to the hospital.

The drill was familiar—Les got prepped; we stayed with him until surgery; Bob and Vicki joined us; the RN led us to the waiting room; the doctor came out an hour and a half later and said everything went well. The tumor was indeed cancer, but did not appear to be invasive. We gratefully thanked him and sighed with relief.

When Les was sufficiently awake, we followed his gurney to his room. Our current store of small talk ran out; we just looked at one another. Les appeared to be tired, so everyone said goodbye and went about their ordinary lives. I stayed.

It was all hauntingly familiar.

My "No Lifeguard on Duty" poem becomes more and more relevant. Les and I realize that we haven't been poolside for some time. Nor are we on a sandy beach with waves lapping at our feet. Maybe somewhere well past the breakwater?

Now I Lay Me Down to Sleep

On a frosty night a month or so later, Les laid his reading glasses on the end table, stood up from his chair, and suggested that we go have our "treat" and get ready for bed. I'd finished my daily crossword puzzles and Sudoku, so I agreed.

We shuffled out to the kitchen, poured frozen blueberries into bowls, and topped them with cereal, sweetener, and milk.

When we finished, Les wheeled his rollator back to the bedroom while I turned out the lights and turned on his oxygen concentrator. It immediately screeched, "I'm here. I'm on. You're okay for the night," and then settled into its steady hum, interrupted every five seconds by a burp.

Les had stabilized to a great extent, even though his health continued to be tenuous. The home exercise program I created for him, after he had recovered sufficiently from his surgeries, had reconditioned him somewhat. We continued to allow ourselves to stay in bed until we'd completed the thirty-minute morning workout. Total ploy. During the evening we took turns pedaling our stationary bike for thirty minutes while we watched the network news. Les had not regained his weight, but he clearly had recouped some strength.

With that structure, our chores, our doctor visits and physical therapy sessions, our many little rituals—burning candles at every meal, facing our recliners toward one another to rub the other's feet, my playing piano while Les did dishes—our days had a sturdy rhythm of happiness.

Our nights...?

Les finished brushing his teeth and we climbed into our marriage bed, our place of comfort, warmth, and love. I thought back to our wedding night when Les gently entered me for the first time, the moment I left my seventeen-year-old self behind and became a wife, the instant I knew that I held his happiness in my hands.

I snuggled closer and understood once again how thankful and amazed I am to have such an appealing man in my bed. How extraordinary and awesome it is for us to be crazy-in-love even now.

As we lay together in the dark, I outlined the contours of his dear face, tested the steady beat of his pacemaker, and pretended he would always be there. As every other night, our enthusiastic kisses relived the chemistry and connection that first jolted us into love.

I told him that I adored him. He said, "Ditto." He said that I was the sweetest girl in the world. I hugged him tighter. We have a secret phrase—NP, NP. Translation: There is *no place* I'd rather be and *no person* I'd rather have with me. He spoke it with conviction and I echoed.

Why does love always mean having to say goodbye?

Goodnight, sweet prince.

Old Times

"What was the name of that song about the birds coming back in springtime?" Les asked at breakfast late in February.

"What?" I set down my fork.

"That song about the birds."

Les proceeded to sing a little tune, some words, some la-la-las. I did not recognize either the tune or the words, but I searched our old 1915 *The Golden Book of Favorite Songs* and there it was on page ninety-one, T*he Birds' Return.*

Old Times. There were many others. Like the day he asked, "Did you ever play *Red Rover, Red Rover* or *Fox and Geese?*"

"Of course, didn't everyone?"

"Well, how about *Spin the Bottle?*" Ah, *Spin the Bottle.* When I was a teenager, we blushed if someone kissed us on the cheek. With sexual mores being what they are in the late 2010s, *Spin the Bottl*e would clearly qualify as an odd, innocent throwback.

Once he recited the names of the cows and horses on the homestead: Big Guernsey, Little Heifer, Short Tits, King, Daisy, Maude....

Sometimes he talks about his parents and ten siblings: how his large family was so poor that they totally ignored Christmas one year; how he went shoeless to school until November; how his father had written *Lester is a good boy* on a wooden board; how dearly he wishes that he had that board.

Other times we relish memories of wonderful trips—staying in the quaint 1793 Quechee Inn in Vermont; loving the condo on Maui; crossing the Arctic Circle in Alaska; ferrying on Sognefjord in Norway; speaking at a conference in Manchester, England; visiting the breathtaking Cologne Cathedral in Germany; riding the fast train from Lyon to Paris; taking a picture of Mozart's piano in Salzburg because we didn't see the sign: No Photographs.

Good memories, but no more gratifying than sitting quietly together and sharing breakfast.

Old age gifts us in startling ways. Our agenda is, of necessity, simplified. I can see the end of the tunnel as to the number of annual physicals I have to schedule or how many more springs we have to hire the lawn aerator man.

We have many ready reasons to stay home when we'd prefer to sit in our chairs—or even when we'd rather go. We can say "no" without guilt to requests to be on committees or help with church work day.

Some of our needs and most of our wants have inexplicably disappeared.

On the other hand, if Keith and Russ continue to visit us twice a year, we can probably count on our fingers how many more times we will see them. If we're lucky, add a toe or two.

We have discovered that even the intensely emotional crises can bring their own peculiar euphoria: We are acutely alive in those terrifying moments. Coping effectively brings its own perverse elation. Crisis strips away the ordinary, the routine, the familiar, leaving a splendid core of gratefulness and love.

Yet, Old Time-y mornings with an aromatic cup of coffee are the foundation of our lives.

Of Course I Had My Shot

Les and I smiled at one another across the table at *The House of Tricks* on ASU's campus in Tempe. We were lucky to be celebrating Keith and David's March birthdays with them. Lucky that Keith had fetched us for spring R & R.

Strings of white lights danced above; a soft breeze wafted through the trees to ruffle our hair; the white tablecloth and dinnerware heightened the glow of the candle in the center of our table. It was perfect. Everything was absolutely perfect. Waves of joy washed over me, as I breathed to myself, "Here comes rejuvenation. Forget rest and relaxation. I'm up for total transformation."

After dinner we drove to the Desert Botanical Gardens to see the much-acclaimed light show. Finally, finally a botanic garden. My heart sang.

Spectacular illumination emphasized remarkable plants. The pieces of stunning Chihuly glass delighted us. The hills around us radiated with spider webs of lights, changing colors from darkest teals to brightest reds to gentle pinks to soft yellows to pale greens to brilliant azures. We gazed in awe.

Kara and the girls skipped along, holding hands. David expertly commandeered Les in his rollator. I rather unexpectedly found it necessary to grab Keith's arm to steady myself on the gravel paths. I also coughed once or twice and wondered, "Why does my chest burn? These hills are not that steep."

When I awoke the next morning I was ill again—coughing until I gagged, vomiting, fever, achiness, and overwhelming malaise that pinned me to my bed.

I rested, but I didn't get better. Kara took me to Urgent Care. As I got out of her car, I swayed in the blazing sunshine, willed my legs to move, willed my head to stop spinning, willed my breathing to ease.

I hated the nose swabbing, but the diagnosis—Influenza A and B—shocked me. As I sat on the examining table fuming, the PA reeled off five medications she had ordered.

I made an executive decision to take none of them until I had phoned Dr. Nelson, who had followed us over a year already and whom we had learned to love. He told me that the Tamiflu was too late; the antibiotic was unnecessary. He couldn't think of any reason for a steroid. Since my cough had improved I didn't need two meds for that. I felt vindicated.

I continued to feel puny and spent a lot of time in bed, but by the time Keith took us back home, I was able to appreciate the two-day road trip.

Russ was coming to visit the following week. We barely had time to go through six weeks of mail, unpack, do laundry, host my overdue meetings and breakfasts, check in with our doctors, and start Les' much ballyhooed Spring's Work. It's easy to tell he grew up on a farm.

Sometimes I think that, considering how hard it is to get ready to leave and how tough it is to catch up when we get home, it almost isn't worth the trip. Then I remember the cozy "cereal time" before bed, the long, leisurely talks over coffee, and how much we love sitting on the patio, watching eagles soar over the saguaro-studded hillside behind the house. We do love Arizona.

We are rested. We are restored. Ready for Les to turn ninety-four.

Ninety-fourth Birthday

My dearest love—

Happy birthday, darling.

As I think of all the years we have spent together and how you were only twenty-four when I met you, I simply cannot comprehend that you are now ninety-four. Ninety-four.

Through all these years you have provided for me, comforted me, loved me, and dared me to be better than I am. You have lent me your strength. When I can't remember the song in my heart, you sing it for me. You are the Rock of Gibraltar around whom I have danced.

But one of your biggest gifts has been your longevity, extending your care and kindness over more years than I had any right to expect. What an unforeseen miracle to have grown old together.

And here you are, regaling me with old stories as we share breakfast, doing the dishes, kneeling to fix the sprinkler system, rollatoring about the house, reading in your chair with your glasses sitting halfway down your nose, wrapping your arms around me, kissing me goodnight, sleeping beside me.

Our life together is sweeter than I could ever have anticipated for myself.

Please know that I will be with you. I will walk every step with you. And if you go first, please wait for me.

Mam'selle

Three O'Clock in the Morning

"How was your night?" Les asked as we began our workout two months later. I hesitated to tell him that I had been awake from three o'clock until five-thirty. I knew how much he wished for me to have slept well.

How could I say that there are days that I despair? Mornings when I'm not sure that I can get out of bed?

How could I say that some days I slog through a mire of muddy clay—thick clumps building up on my Mary Jane's, each step becoming heavier, until darkness rescues me as I shake off my shoes and crawl into bed?

How could I complain to this man who already feels as if he is a burden, who grieves his loss of self so mightily, who would give anything to take care of me?

"I couldn't sleep," I said.

His voice was gentle as he prodded, "And what were you thinking about?"

I stopped right in the middle of a cycle of leg lifts and rolled to face him. My words tumbled out.

"I've managed to get most of the maintenance things done, but the yard isn't mulched and the basement bathroom needs to be painted. The bill for our homeowner's policy is too high so I need to check some other companies. I have to call our credit card company about a charge that's wrong."

I told him that on top of all that, I worry about how hard it is to stay on the same page when he can't hear me and I'm too tired to talk loudly or clearly enough for him to understand. How sometimes I think he tunes out on purpose. How our marriage suffers because it is too much of a hassle to even bring up a subject. Obviously we could check into hearing aids, but he keeps saying no and I see that as another set of appointments, decisions, and aggravations.

I stopped to take a deep breath. Dare I go on?

"I really do want to be kind and caring to you, to have superhuman patience. But I don't. Aside from being exasperated that you can't hear me, some days I blurt out snide comments that make you feel like an idiot. Sometimes I insist that you do things you can't do, not accepting that you really can't do them. And I always feel sad when I'm not as supportive as I'd like. I apologize, but how I wish I needn't."

I went on to say how I can't stand seeing him stoop and shrink, even as I hate nagging him about standing tall. I detest quibbling about medications. I want to yank him back from being my patient to just being my stalwart husband again.

I explained how I feel that slipping into the patient and caregiver roles, even as we must, taints our function and connection as husband and wife.

How, though it is hard, I try to quash my anger and irritation for the sake of his comfort and wellbeing. As a caregiver, it doesn't much matter that stuffing my negativity also dampens positive feelings.

But, as a wife, tamping resentment matters a great deal. Our relationship has always been built on honesty and trust.

When either of us represses destructive feelings, we also suppress our love. And little barbs of hostility tend to dart out, anyway.

"None of this is your fault. Or mine. But it's up to me to keep us comfortable and safe. When I'm afraid, I can't sleep."

All my frustration, all my fear poured out.

Les put his arms around me and said, "Oh, my sweet girl. I'm really, really sorry. I know it's hard. I know I lapse into helplessness because it's easier. But nothing you do or say will ever stop me from loving you. We'll get through this together. And next time, please, please wake me so I can be with you here in the dark."

I sighed. I have spent so much time trying to protect Les that it was truly a moment of grace to open the floodgates, to share my blackest state of mind, to have him understand and comfort me. He is my husband. He remembered that he is. He did what only he can do.

Dinner and a Movie

The weather on the Monday that marked our sixty-eight wedding anniversary was in no way reminiscent of the beautiful September day on which we were married.

Gray clouds hung low in the sky and mist darkened the concrete of our driveway. Les groused that he was short of breath and wobbly. He bemoaned the fact that he had done nothing in preparation for our special day. Couldn't we please just ignore it? After breakfast he sat in the bedroom in his recliner, looking glum.

My heart sank. September 12 has always been magical for us: a day hung with glistening streamers; a day outlined by glitter; our day brimming with delight, memories, and infinite pleasure.

I had been uneasy for a month or two, as I often am before a birthday, wedding anniversary, or other significant occasion, praying that we would actually reach sixty-eight years. And we had. Celebration was in order.

As I read the newspaper, I looked over at my dear husband, who was sad that he couldn't plan, unhappy at his lack of energy and resources, dejected as he faced the day.

But we would not let the day pass just sitting in our chairs, with the forbidding sky and over-leafed trees so darkening the room that we could not see without turning on every lamp.

I did up the chores, checked my multitude of emails, then announced, "You need to shave and shower. We are leaving the house at one-thirty."

Les beamed as I backed out of the driveway. He loves surprises. We held hands in the theater as we watched *Sully*, the movie about Captain Sullenberger's heroic landing on the Hudson River in New York City. Les kissed me as we rose from our seats and said, "I loved it. I absolutely loved it. Thanks. I needed that."

The clouds and gloom had burned off; the sun shone brightly as we walked to the car. It kept shining as we had a nice early dinner, topped off with our favorite hot fudge sundaes.

We did the expected; we celebrated; we had a fine time. But throughout the movie, even during the part when our fellow movie-goers let out their breaths and applauded because everyone was safely off the plane and on land, our own hearts quietly broke. If only we could exhale. Our anniversaries, happy for them though we may be, are a little tinge of pink on the edges of a stormy sky.

Nevertheless, we understand that there has been as much wonderment, as much enlightenment, in the challenging moments of our lives as in the sublime. In the eight years since our sixtieth, we have journeyed from vitality to infirmity, from strength to weakness, from relative innocence to the fierceness of deep awareness.

Parallel universes, foreign lands, and a curious lack of lifeguards....

Christmas 2016

*M*y dear Mam'selle –

For several years, I've feared each Christmas could be our last. But even after bladder cancer, here is another one. Your devotion these past years has made me ever more thankful for you. Tears fall when you tell me that you will take care of me always, no matter how difficult it gets.

I am amazed at the luck I had when I attached myself to that young, innocent girl—a decision I have never regretted.

A love that started as a dream-come-true has grown into something unimaginable. We have been beyond fortunate. My love for you has been part of why I have lived this long.

When I cuddle with you at night or gaze at you at breakfast, my heart is filled with gratitude for that wonderful person who is you.

The very idea of leaving you breaks my heart. You are the best thing that ever happened to me and my love for you will never end.

Les

The Precise Moment

I believe that life is made precious
by the fact that we will die
that mortality illuminates our temporal existence

These years of illness and aging have brought
the clarity of finely cut glass
to the days going forward

I hunger to etch your every expression
into my memory
your every gesture into my heart

It is the precise moment in which
we concede our transience
that life and love become most cherished

We Can See the Trees

One morning in early January I wrestled the unwieldy recycle bin to the curb as I skidded around in the snow. I lifted the heavy trash bag onto the outdoor rollator and pulled it across the slippery driveway, just as I have every Wednesday since Les has been ill. I knew my back, knees, and shoulders would ache that night.

As a child, I'm sure I never gave a thought to old age. My great-grandfather had seemed quite competent, although I do remember that he sat in his chair most of the time. As an adult, I didn't think much about old age, either.

I certainly could never have imagined my brawny husband unable to set out the trash.

When I returned to the house and sat down to rest, Les and I talked about some of the adjustments we have made to accommodate our old age. We didn't make them all at once, primarily because the solutions didn't occur to us in a timely fashion.

We bought two rollators, a transport chair, and a light-weight walker.

We moved our queen bed six inches north so Les can get nearer to the closet with his rollator. We eliminated an end table in the living room so said rollator doesn't bang the rocking chair. We hung grab bars in five places.

I set up automatic payments for most of our bills. I use QuickBooks to keep track of our finances and make tax time easier. We try to limit our credit charges, so I don't have to post as many entries.

On laundry day, we place the basket on the indoor rollator seat and Les wheels it to the stairway. Then, holding tightly to the railing, I carefully bump the basket down, one step at a time. I wait until someone strong comes to the house to carry it up.

Recently I moved the butter dish, peanut butter jar, and sugar bowl to a cupboard that is five steps closer to the toaster. Five steps. I tossed out the mason jars that held things I wouldn't use in a million years, such as stale buckwheat flour. I got rid of most of my plastic containers. The microwave gets more use than the glass stovetop or the oven. My mother would be horrified.

And we pushed the table to the middle of the kitchen, closer to the counters, so it is more easily set and cleared.

We had often longed to be able to see outside while we were eating. There is only one window in the kitchen; it faces a brick wall. It took all these years to realize that if we moved the table, we could see through the arch and out the large living room window. We could see the aspen trees green in the spring. We could see them turn golden. We could watch it snow. All it took was moving the table a measly four and a half feet.

As we make these adjustments, we wonder when they will become insufficient. At some point maintaining our veneer of normal may cause too much stress. We may have to give up the three Christmas trees, the handy laundry in the basement, and the nearby garage. And we are well aware that it could happen in a second.

We also know that we have been favored with more normal than most people, favored mightily through no credit of our own. Same table. Same house. Long lives. Same spouse. Sometimes we almost feel indicted by our good fortune.

For now, we simplify; we streamline; we re-create. We continue to revel in the scented white candle that flickers between us during each and every meal.

Nothing Left to Say

We sit across the breakfast table.
"How was your night?"
"How did YOU sleep?"

Spoons dip into warm oatmeal.
Eyes meet—you wink at me
I wink back and smile.

"Did you read that article yesterday?"
"The one about the pipeline?"
"No, the one about that awful accident."

We sip in peaceful silence
then go about our day—
after all these lovely years
nothing left to say.

But when we go to bed at nine
you turn to me—your lips find mine.
No need for words.

Arizona Once More

Keith flew to Denver in February to drive us to Mesa. Another beautiful trip. Another long, contented stay in our comfortable suite.

One afternoon Kara took us to Saguaro Lake for a special outing. The seventeen-mile drive from their house was lined with exquisite paloverde and forests of saguaro. The lake, rimmed by rock canyon walls, lay calm and as beautiful a blue as ever. It reminded us of the many picnics we had there with Ralph and Mary Jo during our multiple visits.

This trip was the fifth of our elongated R & R's. We have grown to love the state even more than we had during our many spring breaks, particularly this corner of it.

Several evenings later, as Keith, Kara, Les, and I sat on the front patio to watch the full moon rise, I felt strange. When I checked my pulse, it was above 120 for about an hour. Five nights later the same thing occurred. Les and I worried, but my heart rate soon normalized. We pretended it hadn't happened; we were resting and restoring, for goodness' sake. No time for ERs.

However, I did have the good sense to mention the episodes to Dr. Nelson when we returned home. He suggested that I wear a monitor for a month to see if we could catch an episode, diagnose whatever, and treat it. I indulged him and wore the uncomfortable contraption. Nothing. Nothing at all.

"But what if it happens again?" I asked at the very next follow-up appointment.

"Go to the ER immediately to see if they can catch something. We can't ignore this. We need a diagnosis," Dr. Nelson had cautioned.

No problem. It wouldn't happen again. And we'd visit Keith and Kara in the fall, of course.

A Moment to Treasure

A month later, Russ was taking Les and me to the Inverness Hotel for Les' ninety-fifth birthday Big Bash weekend when snowflakes began to hit the windshield. Yay! A spring snowstorm. How fun to have a snowy weekend for the party.

The snow intensified through the celebratory dinner with our children and spouses that evening, continued all night, through our delightful breakfast, and on into Saturday. That afternoon we all worked on the quiz I had made: ninety-five questions that turned out to be a thorough review of Les' life from his childhood on the homestead, his athletic prowess, his WWII Navy experience, to all the years of our marriage.

The snow continued to pile up. The landscape transformed into a fairyland of pure white. Deep, pure white. It snowed all through dinner Saturday night, too.

Our table for eight was next to a huge window. The unexpected beauty heightened our pleasure in being together. It was one of the happiest occasions of my recent life, even as we all grappled with the reality of Les having turned ninety-five. What a gift it was. What a bonus. What a bewilderment.

I kept telling myself, "Stay in this exquisite moment. Just stay in the moment."

Put on Your Shoes

We had finished dinner on the Friday of Memorial Day weekend. Les had settled himself in front of the TV, ready for the CBS *Evening News*. As I walked through the den toward the bedroom, my rib cage thumped. The oximeter registered a heart rate of 150. I yelled, "Put on your shoes. We're going to the ER right now."

I tied his shoelaces, picked up my purse and car keys, and drove the four blocks to Porter ER. Note to self: Next time call 911.

We caught the diagnosis, all right. It took three hours to get my atrial fibrillation under control. Karen and Les watched in consternation as the heart monitor zigzagged uncontrollably.

Les and I settled into the hospital. The fact that I was in the bed and he slept on a cot distressed me greatly. I did the best I could to take care of him, even with IVs dangling and gown falling off my shoulders. I requested a blanket and pillow for him, ordered our meals, and reassured him that everything would be all right. I wasn't certain I believed that. I worried that I would go down the same a-fib road he had, right into heart failure. I wept quietly, so as not to wake him.

We went home after three days. All throughout June I tried to get used to the same medication that Les hadn't tolerated four years ago. I couldn't. It made me too ill. I carry a pill in my pocket, too.

My new chronic illness shocked me. My health has shifted, but nothing has changed about my caregiver role. Questions— Can I continue? For how long?—beleaguer me. An additional blanket of unease sits on my shoulders.

All Packed Up, Ready to Go

By the middle of July, I was barely recovered from the medication side effects when a nasty virus laid me low. I had to convalesce quickly—our granddaughter Lyndsey and her fiancé, Matt, were getting married in Michigan in three weeks.

Bob and Vicki planned to take us. Dr. Nelson had cleared both Les and me for the trip. I packed our suitcases a week early and set them in the garage. We could scarcely contain our excitement.

Two evenings before our departure, Karen and Emily came for dinner. They had shopped for me and brought four jackets to try. I wanted to spruce up the long navy dress I planned to wear for the main event. And hide my wrinkly arms.

The three of us laughed and giggled as I tried on each one. Les watched the Rockies and gave thumbs-up or -down as I modeled.

One remarkably beautiful silver jacket, well-sequined, was perfect.

Oh, Shit

Anticipation woke us early the next morning. Only one more day. As I snuggled close to Les, his skin seemed warmer than usual. I took his temperature. One hundred degrees. Oh, shit.

I fretted and cried. I tried to think of alternate plans. There weren't any. Our trip was off. We would not see Lyndsey marry Matt.

That evening, as I prepared to take Les to the ER, temperature now over 102°, he collapsed in the hallway. He clutched at the door jamb, hands slowly slipping, legs giving out. I gently lowered him to the floor, carefully stepped over him, and called 911.

A firetruck squealed up. Four burly men burst into the house and began pushing furniture aside. An ambulance pulled to the curb with another four hefty men who crowded into the narrow hall.

Les was admitted to Porter with a severe UTI and sepsis. Then he got pneumonia in his right upper lobe. Then he got pneumonia in both lower lobes.

Les went into delirium early on. He seemed lucid only about ten percent of the time. His temperature continued to spike. In the middle of the night, he would yell and rant about a dentist bill or try to fix a connection, which was not broken, on one of his many IV lines. He threatened to "call the cops" on the nurses. I got up from my cot many times to try to calm him, to rub his legs, to comfort him.

The doctors administered courses of five different antibiotics. Nothing seemed to work. I did not see how he could survive. I prayed that he would at least live until after Lyndsey's wedding.

I did not go home for ten days. Karen and my sister dug into my packed suitcase and brought fresh clothes; I showered in Les' bathroom. I ordered meals, then fed Les because he was too weak to hold a fork. I greeted visitors and talked softly in the hallway. I picked a skilled nursing facility out of the four my sister scoped out for me, even though no one was sure that Les would ever leave the hospital.

I put one foot in front of the other and wondered each night if his mind would clear enough that I could talk with him once again. I feared I might awake to widowhood.

I had never felt more alone.

The Puzzle

"You need to pack up your things. The transport van will be here in forty-five minutes to move Les to rehab," the case worker said, "and you will have to leave then, too." All of a sudden. Just like that?

I knew that things had been improving incrementally, but Les' pneumonia had not resolved. When the idea of moving him to a skilled nursing/rehab center had first been broached a number of days earlier, I said, "Absolutely not. They say I can't stay with him there, so absolutely not."

As the days had gone by, however, it became increasingly clear that I couldn't take care of him at home. He could barely get out of bed. His mind was a jumble most of the time.

The hospitalist had said just that morning that maybe Les would be transferred in a day or two, but now I had no choice except to quickly help him dress and pack our accumulated belongings and medical gear.

Life Care Center of Littleton was beautiful—amazing artwork, impressive tapestry draperies, squeaky clean floors, and soft lighting. Warm. Welcoming. Awesome.

But after I kissed Les goodnight, I cried all the way home. We had not been apart in over four years; I had never left the house unless he came along; I had always awakened next to him. That night I slept alone in our bed, shivering cold after one of the hottest days of the season, imagining how it would be if I never brought him home, and continuing to brace myself.

The next morning, as I hurried through Life Care's lobby, I glimpsed a side table with a 1,000-piece puzzle, the edges solidly in place, many of the pieces sorted into piles of various colors.

Three residents in wheel chairs—a dark-haired man with a scruffy beard, a woman whose spine was so crooked that her face almost touched the table, and a partially paralyzed young man—were scrutinizing the jumble intently, occasionally picking up a piece and turning it in their hands.

Another time I examined the picture more closely. A reddish orange bowl seemed to be developing right and lower center. Some flowers were half-formed. The edges retained their firmness. As usual, three, not always the same three, but three, residents were concentrating on their work.

A week or so later I stopped by again and saw that the red bowl was less formed, not more. Some of the flowers had disappeared. Some of the neatly stacked color piles had scattered. One of the edges was breached. The puzzle was undoing.

Had the man, the woman, the boy, the others given up? Were any of them truly trying to get the puzzle together? Or were they attempting to figure out the fragments of their lives, only to realize that they could not?

In my innermost being I knew that puzzle would never be completed.

This past summer, those illnesses clarified our existence in a way nothing else had. Les and I have come to see our lives a bit like that puzzle. We imagine we have our pieces properly sorted, the colors organized, but the picture dissolves before our eyes.

My dearly loved husband is slowly recovering, but it won't be to where he had been, even with the upcoming five weeks of home health care. With each incident he loses a little more stamina and resilience. I continue to hang by my fingertips.

We will not go to Arizona this fall. In all likelihood we will never go again.

But I can see that in facing our setbacks, in trying to solve the puzzle, we have changed, tempered. There will be further difficulties; nonetheless, they no longer seem like unmitigated catastrophes. We do not need to panic; we have trod this ground before. Our love strengthens as it is tested. Our fortitude magnifies as we go forward. One of us will die sooner than the other. We are resolute, if not ready.

The crazy, random pieces of our lives are not likely to fall into place, but they are still colorful and it still behooves us to try. Is incumbent upon us to try.

To pick them up in our hands and turn them gently.

Saturday Morning

I unwind like a cat, stretch, and snuggle back to luxuriate under our comforter. I am glad that Les has returned home, that the twenty-some home health care visits are finished; happy that Les' mind is mostly clear and that he is gaining stamina; pleased to recuperate after a busy week.

Les stirs and turns to face me.

"Hi," I whisper.

He draws me onto his body for an extended nuzzle. I so love the feeling of his long beautiful limbs entwined with mine.

We do our exercises, now stretched to forty minutes. As we complete one cycle, I swing my right leg from side to side while Les grips my left wrist so that the heavy ankle weights won't yank me out of bed. I laugh and say, "Wouldn't it be funny if I fell over the edge and yanked you off on top of me? The kids would discover us, cold and dead, and wonder what the heck we'd been doing." Well, maybe not *that* funny.

I slip into my robe and slippers and pad out to the kitchen. I turn on the coffee pot and warm our plates. I heat the skillet, pour orange juice, whip up pancake mix, and break three fresh eggs.

When I set his plate in front of him, Les says, "I love Saturdays. I love the way you do eggs. I love pancakes. I love *you*."

We sit here in the comfort of our kitchen, once again delighting in our treasures—the Daisy butter churn from my grandmother, Grandma Hjelmstad's sparkling cut glass sugar bowl, the pewter teapot Les gave me the first Christmas after I was diagnosed with breast cancer.

As he does every Saturday when we near the end of our breakfast, Les offers me a "lastie"—the luscious center of his prized pancakes, rich with butter and Vermont maple syrup. And as always, I thank him heartily and tell him that he is the sweetest man in the world.

Then we push our chairs close to the glowing warmth of the fireplace, knees touching, and reflect on the goodness of our days. We may go into that Dark Night kicking and screaming, but we have been together more than seventy years. Nothing can take that away.

Les asks, "May I have a smidge more coffee?"

I smile, "Of course, my love." I fetch the pot and pour rich, steaming brew into his outstretched mug.

We are here. We are together. It is enough.

Resources

Books

Callanan, Maggie and Patricia Kelley. *Final Gifts: Understanding the Special Awareness, Needs, and Communications of the Dying*. New York: Bantam, 1997.

Gawande, Atul, MD. *Being Mortal: Medicine and What Matters in the End*. New York: Metropolitan Books, 2014.

Kubler-Ross, Elisabeth and David Kessler. *On Grief and Grieving: Finding the Meaning of Grief through the Five Stages of Loss*. New York: Scribner, 2014.

St. James, Elaine. *Simplify Your Life: 100 Ways to Slow Down and Enjoy the Things That Really Matter*. New York: Hachette Books, 1994.

Shultz, Lisa J. *A Chance to Say Goodbye: Reflections on Losing a Parent*. Breckenridge, Colorado: High Country Publications, 2017.

Websites

www.aarp.org/caregiving/families   888.687.2277
www.agingwithdignity.org
www.caringinfo.org
www.davidkessler.org
www.mydirectives.com
www.nhpco.org

Acknowledgments

I offer my heartfelt gratitude to my editor, Barbara Munson, and my cover and interior designer, Nick Zelinger, for augmenting my vision, making the book beautiful, and keeping me steadfast and calm.

My deep appreciation also to:

– those who read early drafts and offered encouragement: Carol Feller, Russ and Nancy Gregory, Judith Macomber, Dr. Mark Andrew Nelson, Connie Shoemaker, Fred Silverman, and Arlo Sonnenberg

– others who gave reassurance and ideas: the staffs at the Englewood Public Library in Englewood, CO, Koebel Library in Centennial, CO, and Tattered Cover Bookstore, Littleton, CO

– the beloved members of my writing group who spent endless hours reading, critiquing, rereading, and lending me inspiration and courage: Lynn Hall, Anne Mahoney, and Esther Starrels

– my cherished family for their significant caring and support; my adored husband for his durable love and astonishing longevity

About the Author

Lois Hjelmstad has authored three award-winning books prior to this one, as well as numerous articles.

She has spoken—in all fifty United States, Canada, and England—more than 600 times.

Lois lives with her husband, Les, in Englewood, Colorado, where she taught music for forty years. Les and Lois celebrated their 70th wedding anniversary on September 12, 2018.

They have four children, eleven grandchildren, eight great-grandchildren, and one great-great-grandchild, plus in-laws. All are much loved.

Her mission is to bring clarity, validation, courage, and solace to others.

Visit Lois at *http://www.loishjelmstad.com*

Request for review

If you liked *Abidance*, or found it helpful, perhaps someone else will, too. A review—wherever you purchased it, at *Goodreads*, or any other review platform—will help others decide if they want to give the book a chance. Thank you!